# THE KIDS CAN HELP BOOK

## By Suzanne Logan

A PERIGEE BOOK

Perigee Books
are published by
The Putnam Publishing Group
200 Madison Avenue
New York, NY 10016

Library of Congress Cataloging-in-Publication Data

Logan, Suzanne.
The kids can help book / by Suzanne Logan.

p.   cm.
Summary: Suggests ways children can make a difference in
their world, such as collecting food or clothing, visiting a
shelter, or participating in a Read-a-thon and lists various
organizations that can use help.
ISBN 0-399-51763-4
1. Social service—United States—Juvenile literature.
2. Charities—United States—Juvenile literature.   3. Helping
behavior—Juvenile literature.  [1. Voluntarism.   2. Charities.
3. Helpfulness.]  I. Title.
HV40.L815   1992          92-17015  CIP  AC
361.3'7—dc20

*Printed in the United States of America*
1  2  3  4  5  6  7  8  9  10

# CONTENTS

Helping the Homeless and the Hungry.................................................2

Helping the Elderly.................................................22

Helping the Sick and Disabled.................................................36

Helping Other Kids in Need.................................................52

Helping the Planet and Animals.................................................67

Getting Started.................................................93

Raising Money.................................................104

Directory of Organizations.................................................113

# IT'S UP TO YOU

Problems, problems everywhere you look. In the newspaper, on TV, knocking on your front door. The homeless, the hungry, dirty air, crime, drugs, other kids in need.

A new kid shows up in class. He's skinny and he doesn't wear a jacket even when it's very cold. At lunch time, when everyone else files into the cafeteria, he is nowhere to be seen.

An elderly woman lives alone. Sometimes she has trouble getting out to do her grocery shopping. Another woman lives in a nursing home. Her eyesight isn't very good and she misses reading books.

A young man in a wheelchair has a hard time getting himself dressed every day; there are a lot of things he can't do on his own, but he wants to be able to take care of himself. What can you do about it?

More than you think. Kids are not powerless. They can help turn the world around. They can make it a better place. This book will tell you how. The rest is up to you.

## SHARE

Share the ideas in this book with your family and friends, your class and your teacher, your club and your neighbors. You can do a lot by yourself. You can do even more with help from your friends.

# Helping the Homeless and the Hungry

# SAY IT WITH DINNER

Homeless people don't have kitchens or stoves. They often don't have enough to eat. Homeless people get their food from soup kitchens or even garbage cans. For many, it has been years since they've had a good home-cooked meal.

Kids at New York's Brearley School are doing something about this. Once a month they prepare a home-cooked meal for the residents of a nearby homeless shelter. They plan the menu, prepare the meal, and deliver it. It's a big responsibility but they're up to it. They know that people at the shelter count on them.

## What You Can Do

Get your club, group, or family to be responsible for cooking a meal once a month for the people in the homeless shelter. (There are big shelters and small shelters; some care for as few as six people, some for hundreds.) You may already know about a nearby shelter. If you don't, there are several ways to locate a shelter in your area:

1. Call the **Coalition for the Homeless**. Most cities have a local branch; they will give you the addresses or phone numbers of shelters in your area. If you can't find a local chapter in your phone book, you can call the national headquarters at (202) 265-2371 and they can tell you the nearest chapter to your hometown.

2. Contact a local branch of the **Salvation Army**; they run many shelters and soup kitchens all over the United States.

3. Call nearby churches or synagogues. Look in the yellow pages of the phonebook under "Churches" and "Synagogues." Chances are that even if the first place you call doesn't operate a shelter, it will give you the phone number of one that does.

Try to call the shelter you've selected around mid-morning. It's the least busy time for people who work in shelters. They will have more time to talk to you, and you won't feel rushed or quite so nervous. (Naturally, you might feel a *little* nervous. You've probably never done this sort of thing before.)

Ask to speak to the person who coordinates volunteer activities. Or if there's nobody who does that, just ask for the person in charge.

To help cut down on nervousness, it's a good idea to write out the things you want to say, things like your age, the name of your club or group, how many kids will be participating in the cooking, etc. It's a good idea to write down your name, too. You'd be surprised how easy it is to forget your own name when you're nervous! Keep the piece of paper beside you when you call so you can refer to it. Keep a pencil handy so you can make notes as the person talks to you. (For more on making phone call, read pages 99-101).

## More Great Ideas

• What if cooking a meal doesn't turn you on, but you make a great chocolate chip cookie? Bake a batch and deliver it to a soup kitchen or homeless shelter. Do this on a regular basis, maybe once a month, or even once a week.

Recruit other kids to bake as well. Get your Scout troop or your Sunday school class into the kitchen and bake up a storm!

You might want to concentrate on after-school snacks for homeless kids. Home-baked cookies are real treats.

• Baking not your thing? Why not volunteer to serve food at a homeless shelter? They're not exactly begging for eight-year-olds, you say. Ask a parent to go with you, then make yourself useful. You'll impress them, I know you will.

*Keep in mind: Who knows better what homeless kids need than other kids? Get your parents or older brother or sister to take you to a shelter—and look at the situation from a kid's point of view.*

# GIVING WARMTH

Homeless people often don't have coats. They don't have gloves, hats, or sweaters either. You can do something about that.

## What You Can Do

1. Look in your closet. There must be an old coat in there, one you've outgrown. What's it doing? Just hanging there. Now start investigating other closets in the house. Go ahead, be nosy, rummage around.

2. Tell your friends to do the same thing in their houses. Before long you'll probably have a pile of coats and sweaters nobody wears anymore.

3. Take the warm clothing to a shelter for the homeless. Or find out if your local church or synagogue can help you distribute your coats to the needy.

There are more ways to make sure the coats get to people who need them.

Organizations like **The Salvation Army**, **Volunteers of America**, and the **United Way** might be able to help you distribute items you've collected. See if there's a local branch near you and call. Tell them you're collecting clothing and would like to have it given to the needy.

If you call the **Points of Light Foundation**, (800) 879-5400, they will send you a booklet of volunteer groups in your area. These groups may be able to help you distribute clothing or other items you've collected. See page 94 for more information on Points of Light.

*Keep in mind: Make sure the coats are clean. If they're not, try to have them professionally cleaned. If you've collected a lot of coats you could tell a local dry cleaner about your project. They might even clean them for free!*

## Another Great Idea

Start a glove drive. It's simple. Anyone can do it. First, gather up all the odd gloves in your house. Then ask relatives and friends to do the same thing. This is what a man in New York did. Before you knew it, he had hundreds of gloves. On Christmas day he took them into the streets and distributed them to homeless people. They didn't care that the gloves didn't match. They were glad to have them. Now he does this every Christmas.

**Great Ways to Collect Clothes**

1. Have your scout troop, class, or club ask local clothing stores for donations of warm clothing.

2. Go door to door in your neighborhood asking for old coats and sweaters. **IMPORTANT: Always get permission from your parents to go door to door, and never go by yourself. And don't go inside strangers' homes—even if it's raining outside.**

3. Ask dry cleaners to donate unclaimed coats. Believe it or not, people sometimes take things to be cleaned and forget all about them! In large cities and towns this can be a major source of warm clothing. Make regular monthly stops at dry cleaners. Soon they'll come to expect your visits.

Ask the dry cleaner to act as a collection center for old coats. What could be more convenient than bringing an old coat to the same place where people take other things to be cleaned? It's an idea whose time has come. You can make it happen.

*Keep in mind: The majority of homeless people are mothers and children. Kids' coats are especially needed. The next time you're tempted to throw your jacket down on the playground, think twice. Treat it gently. Somebody out there is waiting for you to outgrow it.*

## SUCCESS STORY

Trevor Ferrel of Pennsylvania started distributing blankets to the homeless when he was 11 years old. Seven years later, Trevor's blanket distribution program has expanded into two shelters for the homeless in Philadelphia and outposts in 15 cities.

# LETTUCE EAT

There are hungry people in your town. They may get food stamps, but toward the end of the month they sometimes run out of stamps. What can **you** do about it?

## What You Can Do

Grow some for them! (Food that is, not stamps.) This is what kids in Montpelier, Vermont, are doing. They plant and tend their own gardens, then donate the harvest to local soup kitchens and food pantries. "Lettuce Eat" is the name they came up with for the garden behind their school building.

The kids in Montpelier have done more than plant a garden, however. They made a year-long study of hunger and its causes, then came up with a citywide plan for feeding all the hungry people in Montpelier. Their plan is to establish school and community gardens where residents can grow their own food.

"Many people say we are just children and should wait until we are older to create anything like this," the kids said at the press conference they gave to announce their findings. "However...it's our future and if we analyze the malnutrition problem now, we'll have the answer well under way soon."

**If you'd like to start a similar food garden in your community, contact Food Works, 64 Main Street, Montpelier VT 05602. Telephone: (802) 223-1515.**

*Keep in mind: You don't have to do a major study to help feed hungry people in your town. If you like to grow things and you have a backyard, you can plant your own garden and give the harvest to a food kitchen.*

Even if you don't have your own backyard, there are other options. Many cities maintain plots of land called community gardens where people can grow vegetables, fruits, and even flowers. To locate one of these gardens in your town or city, look in the white (or blue) pages of the local phone book under "City Government Offices;" then look for the subheading "Parks and Recreation." Call the number. (Don't forget that little trick about writing down what you want to say.)

What if your town doesn't have land set aside for growing things? Don't give up! Ask if they'd be willing to help you or your group find some.

Or see if your school has some land you could use. It could become a great school project. It's educational, too; learning about growing things is part of studying science.

# SCOUTING FOR FOOD

What better place to collect food for the hungry than a supermarket? This is what the **Boy Scouts of Greater New York** do.

Every year before Thanksgiving, they cruise the aisles of supermarkets handing out leaflets asking shoppers to donate food to the hungry.

The leaflets list the kinds of food needed, like peanut butter; tuna fish; canned soups, fruits, and vegetables; cereal; baby formula; dried beans and pasta; and rice. Fresh foods such as cheese, vegetables, and milk spoil too quickly.

At the exit, more Boy Scouts stand by to bag the items, which are then sent to a community-based food pantry for distribution to the city's hungry.

## What You Can Do

Start a similar food drive in your community. You can also ask local supermarkets to consider matching shoppers' donations. The New York Boy Scouts got several local supermarket chains to agree to this. As a result, they collected 200,000 containers of food. Wow, that's a lot of food!

If you want to know more about how to start a food collection program in your community, contact Boy Scouts of America, 135 West Walnut Hill Lane, P.O. Box 152079, Irving, TX 75015-2079. Telephone: (214) 580-2000.
Or see page 119 for other organizations involved in distributing or collecting food for hungry people.

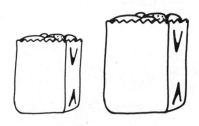

# More Great Ideas

• Take the food drive into your parents' workplace. Set up collection bins in stores, banks, movie theaters, and schools. People have been collecting food for the hungry this way for years.

• Take a friend or two and go door to door in your neighborhood. On your first visit, explain what kind of food is needed and leave containers or shopping bags to put it in. The following week, go back to collect it. (Be sure to smile and say thanks.)

*Keep in mind: Hungry people are hungry all year long, not just on holidays. Any time of year is a good time to start a food drive.*

**Need Help Finding Out Who to Give the Food To?**

Ask the local chapters of the **Salvation Army**, **Volunteers of America**, **Coalition for the Homeless,** or **Second Harvest**, an organization that provides food to homeless shelters, soup kitchens, and church groups with meal programs.

Many churches and synagogues have a "Food for the Hungry" type of program. Call and see if you can bring them the food you've collected for distribution. If the church or synagogue you attend doesn't have one, maybe you can help them get one started.

# A ROOF IS A NECESSARY THING

Suppose you and your family didn't have a place to live. You were willing to build your own house, but you didn't know how. More important, you didn't have the money to buy the materials.

**Habitat for Humanity** decided to do something about this. They started a program to help poor people build their own houses. Habitat for Humanity supplies the know-how, the materials, and the volunteers necessary to get the job done.

It's the most amazing thing! Sometimes entire houses are built in a week!

## What You Can Do

You don't have to be an adult or even a skilled carpenter to volunteer. But by the time you're through, you'll probably know a thing or two about hammering and sawing. That's what happened to 14-year-old Cynthia Romain. Last summer she and 183 other kids spent four weeks weatherproofing houses for low-income residents in Kansas City. "Before I did this I wasn't very good with my hands," Cynthia says.

She is now. Cynthia can insulate, caulk, and weatherstrip almost anything. She has also decided on her future career. Cynthia wants to be an architect.

**For information on how to volunteer, contact Habitat for Humanity, 419 West Church Street, Americus, GA 31709-3498. Telephone: (912) 924-6935.**

*Keep in mind:* You don't have to be a teenager to help. Young kids have helped build houses for Habitat with their family. They can help paint walls, fetch tools, and perform other small tasks. And, if you're unable to help in the actual construction of a house, you could get a group of kids together to raise money for some of the materials that go into houses built by Habitat for Humanity. A little money goes a long way. For example, $20 is all it takes to buy lumber for one wall.

So get busy. Put on a show! Collect cans! Have a bake sale! You can help get homeless people off the street and into their own homes. (For more ideas on how you and your group can raise money, see page 108)

*Important fact:* In 1991 Habitat for Humanity built 1700 houses for poor families in the United States and another 1800 in other countries like Africa, India, and South America.

# YOU MUST HAVE WONDERED...

What's it like to be homeless? To sleep in a shelter? To eat in a soup kitchen? To ask for food stamps?

Some 8th graders at the Challenger Middle School in Colorado Springs, Colorado, decided to find out. They organized weekly trips to community agencies involved with the homeless. This included visits to a City Council meeting, a food stamp office, a Red Cross shelter, and a local soup kitchen.

By the time the kids had completed the project, they knew a lot about homelessness. They were also ready to do something about the problem. Some volunteered to serve in a food kitchen. Others organized food and clothing drives. They also talked to their parents about what they were learning and got them involved. And they won an award for their school: the Colorado Governor's Volunteer Award. That was a great day!

**If you would like to know more about how the Challenger School kids organized their project on the homeless, contact Youth Service America, 1319 F Street, NW, Suite 900, Washington, DC 20004. Telephone: (202) 783-8855.**

## Another Great Idea

"Adopt" a shelter. Make friends with the people living in it. This is what a group of kids at the Prairie Middle School in Aurora, Colorado, did. They visited a homeless shelter in their community. They got to know the people, their problems, and the kinds of basic things they needed, like shampoo, diapers, and toothpaste.

The kids started collecting these things in their community and distributed them to the people at the shelter. They also assisted in the shelter day-care room, taking care of small children while their parents were out looking for jobs. When you come right down to it, that's probably the most useful thing a kid can do for homeless people. Because if parents get jobs, they will be able to move themselves and their children out of the shelter and into their own homes, and buy their own shampoo, toothpaste, and diapers.

# HOMELESS KIDS—IT'S CRAZY, BUT THEY THINK IT'S THEIR FAULT

You really feel sorry for homeless kids. Maybe you think there's one in your class, but you're not sure. Homelessness is hardly something a kid brags about.

Or maybe you don't actually know any homeless kids, but you'd like to do something to make their lives a little easier.

## What You Can Do

• In the case of any homeless kids in your class, you can go out of your way to befriend them. Invite them to play with you and your friends at recess. But don't stop there. Include your new friends in after-school activities or ask your parents if you can invite them home to dinner.

After dinner, you might offer to do your homework together. Kids who live in shelters don't have a quiet place to study. Even more important, encourage your new friend to stay in school. Some kids living in shelters stop going to class because nobody seems to care if they learn or not.

• What can you do about the homeless kids you don't know but want to help anyway; how can you find out where they are?

By now you know the answer to that. Call the **Coalition For the Homeless**, the **Salvation Army**; call churches and synagogues.

Once you've located the kids you want to help, don't just barge in. First talk to the people who are responsible for caring for them. Some kids don't want people to know they are homeless. This is especially true of kids in temporary shelters for battered and abused children. Some of them even think it's their own fault that they landed there.

If the people in charge of the shelter think you'd be welcome, then get hopping. Plan parties and after-school art projects. Collect books and set up a book corner, a quiet place where a kid can curl up and read.

If, however, the people who run the shelter think you had better stay away, you can still do something to help. You can make crafts projects— little gifts for the boys and girls. Some of these kids have had a very hard life. This may be the first time anyone has ever given them anything.

You can also raise money so that the kids in shelters can go on recreational outings—to the movies, or the zoo. Even if you never meet them, they'll know somebody cares about them and it will make a big difference in their lives.

*Keep in mind: Some amusement parks and movie theatres let groups of homeless kids in for free, but they usually don't provide free refreshments. You and your group might raise money for a special treat for each kid. After all, what's a movie without popcorn?*

**The Girl Scouts are presently starting several programs to help homeless kids. One involves bringing homeless girls into Girl Scout troops. Another deals with some of the specific social problems homeless kids experience. For more information, contact Girl Scouts of the U.S.A., 830 Third Avenue, New York, NY 10022. Telephone: (212) 940-7500.**

# THE MAGIC OF BOOKS FOR HOMELESS KIDS

Do you like to read? What if there were no books in your home? That's what it's like for many kids who live in homeless shelters.

**Reading Is Fundamental** (RIF) decided to do something about it. They started a program called Open Book to make sure that kids in homeless shelters get the chance to become readers and own books. For kids who have lost their home, the special magic of an open book, of something that belongs to them, can help them to feel better.

## What You Can Do

You and your class or club can help raise money for Reading Is Fundamental's Open Book Program. One way to do this is have your parents, teacher, or school librarian help you organize a Read-a-Thon or Book Auction.

Ask an adult to help you organize a group of kids (the more the better) to participate in the Read-a-Thon.

1. Get friends and neighbors to give you pledges of money for every book you read over a three-month period.

2. Read as many books as you can and keep a list.

3. After everyone has collected their pledges, hold a book party inviting people to help you celebrate and plan other ways to continue raising money for Open Books.

Another fun way to raise money is a Book Auction.

1. Write to authors of kids' books and ask them to donate a few signed copies of their books. You can write to authors by sending letters to the publishing companies that publish their books. The publishers will forward the letters to the authors.

2. Keep writing until you have collected about 25 books or more. The more the better.

3. Invite other kids and their parents to the auction. Make posters and hang them up at school to announce the event.

4. You might ask any authors who live close-by to attend. They could be the celebrity auctioneers.

**For more information on the Open Book Program, contact Reading Is Fundamental, 600 Maryland Avenue, SW, Washington, D.C. 20560. Telephone: (202) 287-3220. Reading Is Fundamental does lots of things for kids. You can write or ask your parent or teacher to write and find out about all the different programs they have.**

## More Great Ideas

• You and your parents, teacher, or club leader can contact a homeless shelter in your community and see if they already have a reading center and need help to keep the project going.

• You could also set up a Saturday Reading Hour where your group, class, or family visit a homeless shelter once a month, bringing with you lots of books to share and leave behind.

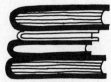

# "EXCUSE ME, WOULD YOU LIKE A SANDWICH?"

I was walking down Park Avenue the other day. Park Avenue is a fine, wide street in New York City lined with big apartment buildings. I was walking along minding my own business when I started to notice all these homeless people. On every block there was at least one. Some looked sad, some looked tired, and a few looked kind of scary. They looked as though they would bite my head off if I smiled and said hello.

I had just passed one of the scary ones when I heard somebody behind me say, "Excuse me, would you like a sandwich?"

I couldn't help it, I turned around and stared. What did I see? A well-dressed man and woman were offering the man a brown paper sack.

I stood there a moment. My heart was pounding. Was the homeless man going to bite their heads off?

No, he wasn't. "Thanks," he said softly, reaching out for the paper sack.

Then I saw that the woman held a canvas bag that contained more brown paper sacks. She and another man were going up and down the avenue, offering lunches to homeless people.

As I started walking again, I tried to picture what was in each of those paper sacks. At least two sandwiches, I hoped, because after lunch comes dinner. And a few carrot sticks, and a piece of fruit, and, of course, a treat. Oreos are what I had in mind.

And that's when I thought, "A kid could do that!" You see, I was already writing this book. What I meant was, a kid could make a bunch of sandwiches and give them to hungry people.

Saturdays would be a good time. You could make them in the morning and hand them out in the afternoon.

**VERY IMPORTANT**: Never do this alone. NEVER! Always go with an adult. Make it a family project. Who knows? Maybe you'll want to do it every week!

# Helping the Elderly

# HIGH TIME

Elderly people can often feel unwanted. Sometimes they may wonder if anybody cares. Kids at the Wyoming Cowboy **Keystone Club** care! They decided that it was high time to show it.

They started giving an annual Christmas dinner for elderly people at their school gym. First, they advertised the dinner at senior citizen centers. They followed the advertisements up with invitations. Then they made arts-and-crafts projects so that every person who attended the dinner would get a gift.

The Keystone Club prepared the food, decorated the gym, and helped their guests get seated. Everybody smiled and ate a lot and had a really great time.

## What You Can Do

There are plenty of holidays other than Christmas that you can celebrate with senior citizens. And you don't always have to cook a whole dinner.

• On Valentine's Day you could bake cookies and serve punch. Be sure that everybody gets a Valentine and be sure its home-made. Home-made Valentines are so much nicer, don't you think? You don't need a big group to do this. You could do it on your own. It will probably be more fun if you could get a couple of friends or your family to come along.

• On Halloween you could serve cider and doughnuts. See if you can get a local bakery to donate the doughnuts. You may have to go to more than one bakery, but if you are polite and explain what you need the doughnuts for, you will probably succeed.

Kids can wear their Halloween costumes. Then while the adults are drinking their cider and eating their doughnuts, the kids can stage a Halloween parade. The adults can vote for the funniest costume, the scariest, the prettiest—you get the idea.

Or you and the senior citizens could carve pumpkins together. Now, there's an icebreaker! Maybe someone in your group could take Polaroid pictures. As your guests leave, hand out the photographs as souvenirs. When they get home, I bet they'll continue to look at them for a long time.

*Keep in mind: You don't have to have a holiday as an excuse for a get-together dinner. Any day of the week will do.*

You'd like to stage a holiday celebration or dinner for elderly people but you don't know where to find them? Here's what you do.

Look in the yellow pages of the phone book under "Nursing Homes" or "Senior Citizen Centers." Also, there is usually a section called "Social Service Organizations" (or "Social and Human Service Organizations"). It lists organizations like the **Salvation Army**, and **JASA (Jewish Association for the Services for the Aged)** that run nursing homes and senior citizen centers.

If there are no such organizations in your town, call local churches or synagogues. They often sponsor homes and recreation centers for senior citizens.

# BE A STAR!

Imagine that you're getting old, but you feel pretty good. And you still get out of the house once in a while. The local senior citizen center is your destination. Bingo is your game. Only those darn bingo chips seem to be getting smaller and smaller, harder to see, harder to pick up.

Enter a group of 6th graders from PS 54 in Queens, New York. The 6th graders spotted the problem. What the senior citizens needed, they decided, were bigger and better bingo chips.

They launched a button campaign. When it comes to buttons, "big and bright" was their motto. And nothing too slippery. They went around the school explaining the need for buttons. They made posters advertising about it and they set up collection centers throughout the school. Then, when they had enough buttons—I'm not sure how many is enough, but it must be hundreds, maybe even thousands—they took them to the senior citizen center. Only they didn't just hand them over. They wrote and performed a rap song first!

But that's not all. At the end of the school year, the 6th graders were awarded StarServe Certificates of Recognition for their "Bingo Button" collection effort. Now that's the kind of thing any kid could do.

There are so many creative things you can do. If you'd like to know how you can help senior citizens in your community and win your own StarServe certificate, contact StarServe, P.O. Box 34567, Washington, D.C. 20043. Telephone: (800) 888-8232. (For more on StarServe, see page 95.)

# MAKING MAGIC

You got talked into it. You and your friends are on your way to visit the nursing home across from your school. You live in the city and the nursing home doesn't look very nice.

Now you're inside. You were right. It *isn't* very nice. And the people in it are kind of weird-looking. Most of them are sitting around in wheelchairs, doing nothing. And then this guy who works in the nursing home walks up and says you're supposed to play volleyball with them!

Now, the residents of the nursing home are being drawn up to a long table. Somebody brings out a beach ball. Teams are made up with an equal number of residents and kids on each team. Well, you're here. You said you'd play, so you do.

At first it's just you and the other kids playing. But soon the residents start to join in. And before you know it your half-hour of play is up.

But wait a minute—you're not done yet. You're supposed to take a name tag and a Magic Marker ("Magic Me" is the name of this project) and go to a resident you'd like to know better. Then you've got to introduce yourself, find out the name of the person, get the correct spelling, and make a name tag for him or her.

Well, maybe you'll come back next week and visit that person again. And maybe that name "Magic Me" isn't so dumb after all. Something magic *did* happen in that room.

**If you'd like to make some magic of your own, write to Youth Service America, 1319 F Street, NW, Suite 900, Washington, D.C. 20004. Telephone: (202) 783-8855. Ask them about the "Magic Me" nursing home project in Baltimore, Maryland.**

## MORE GREAT IDEAS

• You could take your pet into a nursing home. Let the residents hold it, pet it, and play with it. Your dog, your cat, your hamster, even your pet snake would probably be welcomed with open arms. (On second thought, maybe you'd better forget the snake!)

• Like to draw and paint? Do art projects with people in nursing homes. Finger painting is fun at any age.

• Organize a singalong. You and your group may start off singing alone but if you sing enthusiastically enough and really get into it, the older people will join in. Maybe you could even get one of them to accompany you on the piano.

Climb every mountain!

# THE GREAT EYE EXCHANGE

Pretend you live in a nursing home. You watch a lot of TV. You watch soap operas, you watch game shows, you watch sitcoms. You're sick of them, but you watch them anyway. You watch them because your eyes aren't good enough to read anymore. Some days you wish you could go out and borrow somebody else's eyes even for only a couple of hours. Just long enough to read a good book.

## What You Can Do

Lend your eyes. Here's the plan. Offer to read to people in nursing homes. But don't just pick out any book. Put some thought into it. Find out the interests of the person you're reading to, then pick a book you'll both enjoy. Because if you're not interested in what you are reading, you won't read well. You'll just put yourself and the person you're reading to asleep.

And that's another thing; do a little preparation before you read. Look over what you are going to read, maybe make a practice run-through. If there are words you don't know how to pronounce, ask somebody—a parent, a teacher, a librarian.

*Keep in mind: Many kids' books are also interesting to adults. Even a beginning-reader's book could be interesting; one about animals or sports, for instance. They're easy to read but include interesting and unusual facts.*

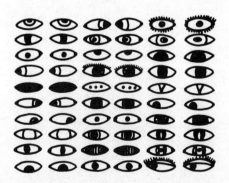

28

It might be fun to ask the person you're going to read to what his or her favorite book was as a kid or the book they liked to read to their kids. Then check it out at the library and take it to your next reading session. I bet it's still around. Books like *Madeleine*, *Winnie-the-Pooh*, *The Secret Garden*, *Little House in the Big Woods*, and *Treasure Island* are classics. They never die.

Also, there are lots of books without words. The idea is to create a story as you look at the pictures. These are great for younger kids who don't know how to read or who are a little nervous about reading to others.

After every reading session, be sure to leave enough time to have a conversation about what you're reading. You might even want to ask the person you're reading to what it was like to be a kid when they were growing up. Which leads me to the next GREAT IDEA. It's really neat, so keep on reading.

# WRITING HISTORY

"Get a life!" You've heard the expression. Well, it's a little hard to do when you live in a nursing home and have to sit around in a wheelchair all day. However, I guarantee that everyone in that nursing home has had a life, probably even a fascinating one! Give it back to them.

Here's how. Write their story. *Who, me?* Yes, you! You go to school, you know how to hold a pencil. It will be fun.

## What You Can Do

Interview your subject. Ask a lot of questions. Don't just ask for facts, like when they were born, where they lived, and whether they lived through any wars, floods, fires—exciting stuff like that—but how they felt about things when they were happening. It may be a little slow getting started, but pretty soon the problem will be writing down the answers fast enough. (A tape recorder is handy for a project like this.)

When you're done asking all the questions, it's up to you to make it into a story. It doesn't have to be very long. A short story can be very effective.

Typing your story isn't necessary; neat printing is okay. And if you like to draw, you can illustrate the story. Whatever you do, make it look professional. Put the pages in a binder or a colorful folder. And don't forget to give your story an interesting title because the right title is very important. Any author will tell you that.

Be sure to make more than one copy. You'll want to have one of your own to share with family and friends after you've given the original to the person whose story you have written. When it's all done, hand it over with a flourish and say, "This is your life!"

*Keep in mind: You really have to get to know the person you're writing about, so one interview won't be enough. You'll have to go back a number of times. But that's the fun of this project—getting to know a lot about somebody you knew nothing about before.*

## Another Great Idea

Not the literary type, but you love to act? Form a **Playback Theater** group.

This is the way it works. You go around to senior citizen centers and ask people to tell you stories about themselves. Then you "play them back"— act them out on the spot. Of course, you'll need a little coaching before you go, and you'll have to learn certain acting techniques.

To learn all about Playback Theater, write to The Community Service Learning Center, 258 Washington Boulevard, Springfield, MA 01108. Telephone: (413) 734-6857. The kids in Springfield have had a Playback Theatre going for several years now. They've made it a big success.

# PEN PALS ARE GREAT PALS

You'd like to visit a nursing home, you really would. But there isn't one nearby and your mom is a single parent. She works hard all day, so she can't take you to one.

## What You Can Do

Write to the people who live there. Here's how you do it. Call a nursing home and ask to speak to the Volunteer Coordinator or the Director of Social Activities. Ask if any of the nursing-home residents would like to receive a monthly letter. Then say you'll call back the next day to find out.

When you call back, you may be given a bunch of names. Don't panic—you don't have to write a different letter to everyone. That's what photocopying machines are for.

In your letter, tell about yourself, your family, the stuff you like to do. You can even tell about the stuff you *don't* like to do, because the person who reads your letter can learn a lot about you when he or she knows what you don't like to do. And learning a lot about you is the point of the letter. Most of the people who want you to write to them don't have much happening in their lives. They're interested in any kind of news.

The important thing is to write regularly. Once you start to write, people will begin to count on your letters. They'll start looking forward to the mail, and when they get your letter, they'll pass it around. They may keep it in their pocket, take it out, and look at it during the day. And every time they do this, I bet they'll smile.

Maybe once a year you can visit the nursing home and meet the people you've been writing to. If you help your mother with some of those things she has to do after work, like cook dinner or wash the dishes, maybe she'll be able to find the time to take you there. Believe me, when you arrive, they'll be lined up waiting to shake your hand. You'll be King or Queen for a day.

*Keep in mind: Each letter should be separately addressed. That makes it seem more personal.*

# IT'S CALLED TELE-CARE

Not all elderly people live in nursing homes. Some live in their own houses or apartments. But a lot of them are lonely, and many of them don't get out much. Sometimes days go by and they have no one to talk to.

## What You Can Do

Call them up. This is what a group of 3rd graders in Polk, Nebraska, have done. Tele-Care is what they call their project.

During their daily calls, each child asks his elderly friend, "Are you okay? Do you need anything?" Most of the time the person assures the student that everything is fine, but sometimes there's a special request. He or she needs medicine delivered, or the front walk needs to be shoveled after a snow storm. When this happens the 3rd grader passes the request along to an adult co-ordinator at a local senior center.

Twice a year, on Halloween at the senior center and at a school tea in June, the 3rd graders and their phone pals meet. These events are always a lot of fun.

**If you'd like more information about how you and your group can start a Tele-Care Program of your own, contact Diane Wurst, Polk Hordville Public School, Box 29, 260 Sough Pine Street, Polk, NE 68654.**

*Keep in mind: You don't have to belong to a program to do this. If you or your family know an older person living alone—maybe the lady down the street or one of your grandparents' friends—you can call them, every day or once a week, to make sure they're all right. Which leads to my next idea...*

# ADOPT-A-GRANDPARENT

Here's a great way to do something super nice for a senior citizen. Is there an elderly person in your neighborhood who doesn't have any family living nearby? Or maybe there's one at your synagogue or church—somebody who usually attends alone. Does your mom or dad know someone who has retired from their work?

## What You Can Do

Adopt them into your family. Make them an honorary grandparent. Visit them on their home turf, invite them to your school assemblies or soccer games. Remember their birthdays. (And remember all those other things—reading to them, writing their life stories, calling to see if they're okay, helping them around the yard—you can do those things, too.) If your parents allow you, you can even invite them into your home for dinner and include them in family holiday celebrations.

You've already got grandparents? That's okay, the more the merrier. Introduce your new grandparent to your real grandparents. That way your adopted grandparent will be making friends his or her own age.

# Helping the Sick and Disabled

# A GIFT OF PUPPY LOVE

People in wheelchairs need special kinds of help and dogs are terrific helpers. They can fetch things, turn on light switches, and even help them take off their socks!

Before these dogs can become companions to people with special needs, they have to be raised to adulthood and given lots of love. And you can do it! Many kids volunteer to raise puppies who will become helpmates to the disabled.

## What You Can Do

Through **Canine Companions for Independence** you raise a puppy until it's 16- to 18- months old. You need to be able to spend a lot of time with your dog, to take it with you when you go places, and even let it sleep in your bedroom. If your school allows, the dog may even go to school with you.

You're responsible for teaching the dog its first commands and taking it to training classes about once a week. You will probably be asked to show off your dog at parades, fairs, and fundraising events.

At the graduation ceremony, puppy raisers hand over their dogs to their new owner. Giving up a dog you raise can be hard. Sadie Stoumen, who is seven, and raised a CCI puppy, agrees. "But I feel good," she says. "Some people have to live without their legs or arms. I only have to live without my dog." Lots of kids keep in touch with their dog's new owner to find out how they're both getting along.

If they live near each other, the puppy raiser is welcome to visit the dog and its new owner. And if the new owner lives far away, there's always the telephone. The dog might not have much to say when you call, but the owner probably will!

The disabled kids and adults who get these dogs feel very lucky. Thirteen-year-old Adam received a labrador and his mother says, "People don't see him as the kid in the wheelchair but the kid with the cool dog." Isolde the dog goes with Adam Short to school, opens doors, picks pencils off the floor, and helps him carry his schoolbooks, but mostly Isolde is Adam's best friend.

If you want to raise a special dog, you'll need your parent's permission and an enclosed yard.

**Write or call the national headquarters to find out about being a puppy raiser: Canine Companions for Independence, P.O. Box 446, Santa Rosa, CA 95402. Telephone: (707) 528-0830. You don't have to live in California; there are puppy raisers across the country.**

# A SPORTING CHANCE

Kids who can't see or who don't have arms or legs or are considered mentally retarded may seem a lot different than you. But they're not. Like all kids everywhere, they like to play games and have a good time. Sometimes, however, they need a little help.

## What You Can Do

Become involved with a group like **Special Olympics**. Special Olympics is a lot like the regular Olympics except it's for handicapped boys and girls. Offer to be a helper at the regional meets that are held all over the country. You might be asked to be a timer, a coach, to hold the finish line tape, or any number of things. Lots of kids and families volunteer at the Special Olympics; and maybe you'll end up going to the national competition.

For more information about becoming a volunteer, contact Special Olympics International Headquarters, 1350 New York Avenue, NW, Suite 500, Washington, D.C. 20005. Telephone: (202) 628- 3630.

## More Great Ideas

• Find out how blind people play baseball. Yes, the blind do play baseball! They use an electronic ball that beeps. That's how they know where it is— they follow the sound. Challenge some blind kids to a game, but don't get too cocky. A group of sighted kids I know who did this got beat!

• Make your own book recording for the blind. Here's what you do. Choose your favorite book. Practice reading it out loud and then record it on cassette. You can also do this as a group. Each of you can take parts. For long books, it's much easier to make it a group effort. Send your tape to a school for blind children. Ask a librarian or teacher there if they'd like more. You could record a whole library of books.

• Visit a center for handicapped kids. Watch the kids at play. See what they are able to do and what they can't do. Then get together with your friends. Figure out how you might adapt some of the games you like to play to the needs and abilities of the boys and girls.

## How to Find Schools and Centers for Handicapped Kids

• Your local school district can give you the locations of any schools for the blind in your area. Your State Board of Education will give you information on the schools for the deaf in your area.

• You can also contact The American Foundation for the Blind. Write to their headquarters at 15 West 16th Street, New York, NY 10011.

• Look in the white or blue pages of the phone book under the heading "Schools" or "Special Education Schools" for schools serving the handicapped.

• Look in the yellow pages of the phone book under "Social Services" for organizations with the words "Blind," "Visually Impaired," "Deaf," or "Handicapped."

• Call one of the volunteer clearing houses on page 94 to find out about organizations in your area that serve the handicapped.

# SUCCESS STORY

On a visit to a center for kids with severe physical handicaps, a group of junior high-school students noticed that the handicapped kids at the center couldn't move around much by themselves. One of the students was really into skateboarding. He wondered if the handicapped boys and girls might be able to use their arms to push themselves along the floor while lying on a low board with wheels.

This sounded possible to the staff at the center. So the boy asked people to give him broken or unwanted skateboards. He got lots of them. Now he is taking them apart and putting them back together, making them wider and adding padded chin rests and straps.

Wouldn't you love to see how much fun those kids will have riding their new skateboards? I bet they'll have a pretty wild time!

# A CLOSER LOOK

Picture this. It's early in the morning. Billy is running out of the house. He has to visit an elderly neighbor before school starts. The neighbor, Mrs. Jones, needs daily eye drops, but she can't administer them herself because she has arthritis. Billy will put them in for her. Billy's friend Kimberly will perform the same service this afternoon on her way home from school.

You wouldn't mind doing something like that? But you don't know anybody who needs eye drops. As far as you know, everybody around you is healthy.

Look again. What about the man who lives in the house around the corner? He's confined to a wheelchair. Last week you saw somebody trying to get him and his chair down the outside steps of the house and having a pretty hard time of it. And then there's the blind girl you sometimes see standing on the corner waiting to cross the street. Or Mr. Harris, your neighbor down the street who just got home from the hospital a few weeks ago. He used to be so proud of his front yard. Now it's starting to look kind of shabby.

## What You Can Do

• Build a ramp for the man in the wheelchair. A couple of junior high kids in Allegheny, Pennsylvania, did this as part of their shop project.

• Offer to help the blind girl across the street. Be sure to talk to her as you cross. And if she's going your way, walk with her and keep talking. By then both of you should be almost over your shyness. Who knows? You just might make a new friend.

• Knock on Mr. Harris's door and ask him if you can clean up his yard. Then keep on doing it until he's well enough to do it himself.

# THE BEST MEDICINE

Nobody likes to be sick, especially if they have to be in a hospital for a long time. When this happens, a person could use a little cheering up.

Most hospitals have lots of ideas about things volunteers can do. All you have to do is call and ask.

## What You Can Do

• Make get-well cards for people in hospitals and convalescent homes. If you don't know anyone who's in the hospital, call your local hospital and ask them if there are any people who don't get any visitors. Ask for the address and send cards to them.

• Bring patients special treats like cookies and candies. But check first to make sure their doctor will let them eat things like that.

• Get your club or church group to visit patients in hospitals. Sing, dance, perform skits, make people laugh. Laughter, they say, is the best medicine. After the show, be sure to go around and talk to as many patients as you can. For most of them, that will be the best part of your visit.

• Become a special "summer friend" to a kid or an adult undergoing long term treatment in a hospital or convalescent home. Visit your friend weekly, and if he or she is still in the hospital when you go back to school, keep in touch through phone calls and letters.

# GERMS AREN'T THE ONLY THINGS THAT ARE CATCHING

You may know a kid who is battling a serious disease. Maybe you were once very sick yourself.

I know a girl who had leukemia. She had to spend a long time in the hospital undergoing treatment, some of which was, as she says, "no picnic." This girl beat the disease. Her doctors were so impressed with her courage that they asked her to come back and visit the other patients. And even though the girl was pretty sick of hospitals, she was happy to do this. You see, she and her doctors knew that germs aren't the only thing that are catching. So is courage.

## What You Can Do

If you have battled a serious illness yourself or are still battling one, you can form a support group for sick kids. Ask your doctor or local hospital to help you get one started. Here's what you do.

1. Ask your doctor if he or she has treated any other kids with serious illnesses. Ask the doctor if he or she can give you the phone numbers and addresses of these other kids. (The doctor will have to check first with the kids and their parents to see if it's okay.)

2. If you do get some phone numbers, call them up and tell them you'd like to get together and talk about what it is like to be sick. Talking to other kids can be a big help. You could also tell your doctor to give other kids who are sick your name and phone number.

3. What does a support group do? Mostly it just listens and shares. You listen to other kids talk about their problems and experiences and you share your own. It can be very comforting to know that you're not alone and that other kids have had the same fears. And when there is good news to report, it's great to have all those people sharing your happiness.

**SUCCESS STORY**

Two girls who live in Chapin, South Carolina, have done more than form a support group. One, Carla Derrick, lost an eye to cancer. The other, Leslie Wilson, lost a lung and a leg. Together they wrote, produced, and directed a video, "How to Cope." The video answers questions kids newly diagnosed with cancer most often ask.

"Cancer changed my life," says Carla. "I don't take life for granted. I try to see some good in everything because there is good in everything...it was the hardest thing that I ever had to go through, and I made it, and I'm not afraid of anything now."

If you'd like to find out more about the "How to Cope" video call (803) 765-6484.

## More Great Ideas

• You don't have to have been seriously ill yourself to help other sick kids. Visit the childrens' wing of a hospital. You may be a little shocked at some of the things you see, and some of the kids may be pretty depressed at first. But by the time you leave, most of them will be smiling.

• There are 22 Shriners' Hospitals for children in the country. They offer free, special medical care to kids. Look in the phone book, call, or write their national headquarters to see if there's a hospital near you. It might be a good place to start!

**Shriners' Hospitals for Crippled Children, P.O. Box 31356, Tampa, FL 33631-3356. Telephone: (800) 337-5055.**

• There are several organizations involved in helping sick kids find the courage to keep on going:
Two of them are the **Make-A-Wish Foundation** and **Starlight Foundation**. A long-hoped for trip to Disneyland, a personal visit from a grandparent who lives three thousand miles away—these are the kinds of dreams that Make-A-Wish and Starlight realize for sick kids. But making dreams come true costs money.

**If you'd like to contribute, contact Make-a-Wish Foundation, 2600 North Central Avenue, Suite 936, Phoenix, AZ 85004. Telephone: (800) 722-9474.**

**Or Starlight Foundation, 12233 West Olympic Boulevard, Los Angeles, CA 90064. Telephone: (310) 207- 5558. You don't have to give a lot of money. As little as a dollar helps.**

Another organization making dreams come true for sick kids is **The Hole-In-the-Wall Gang Camp**. The camp is in Connecticut. It's for severely disabled or ill boys and girls who would not otherwise get an opportunity to attend camp.

If you'd like to contribute, contact The Hole-in-the-Wall Gang Camp Fund, Inc., 555 Long Wharf Drive, New Haven, CT 06511. Telephone: (203) 772-0522.

# WALK FOR HEALTH

In some countries, kids get sick because the water they drink is contaminated. And when they do get sick there are not enough doctors or medicine to help them get well. What can you do about it?

It's pretty simple. All you have to do is go on a long walk and raise money. It's called a walk-a-thon.

**Project Concern International** led the first walk-a-thon ever in the United States—way back in 1969.

Project Concern International is a terrific organization dedicated to providing health care to kids who ordinarily wouldn't get any. Project Concern immunizes poor kids all over the world against all kinds of terrible diseases, as well as teaches their mothers how to care, feed, and house them so that they are less likely to get sick. It also addresses the root cause of many diseases in underdeveloped countries—contaminated drinking water—through the construction of safe wells.

One way Project Concern International raises money to do all of these great things is through its Walk for Children Program. Actually, *walks* for children is a better way of defining them, because Project Concern sponsors walks in over 40 cities every year.

One of its most popular walk-a-thons is the Wee Walk. This is a 5K route (that's five kilometers, or about 3.1 miles) especially designed for kids ages two through eight. There are also walks for older kids.

If you'd like to find out if there is a Walk for Children in your community, contact Project Concern International, 3550 Afton Road, San Diego, CA 92123. Telephone: (619) 279-9690.

*Keep in mind*: Project Concern International allows walkers to give 20 percent of the money they raise to local charities or causes. The cause need not relate specifically to health. Walkers can designate their share of the money to churches, service clubs, youth organizations—just about any cause or group they like.

# BLANKETS FOR BABIES

Remember that blanket you had when you were little? You dragged it everywhere. That blanket was a real friend. It comforted you when you were sick or sad and lonely.

Four women in Berkeley, California, decided to make handmade quilts for AIDS babies. They took their idea into local schools. Soon 2,000 kids were quilting up a storm. Most of them had never quilted before. A lot of them didn't even know how to sew. But they had fun learning. And the quilts they turned out were gorgeous! Within a year they had made 400 quilts, and distributed them to AIDS babies.

Guess what? The babies really love their quilts. Says one foster mother who cares for AIDS babies, "I have one little two-and-a-half year old whose quilt is in tatters. He drags it everywhere. They've offered to make him another, but he refuses."

**The quilt project has gone nationwide. If you'd like to find out how to start one, contact Children's Quilt Project, 1478 University Avenue, Suite 186, Berkeley, CA 94702. Telephone: (510) 548-3843.**

# Helping Other Kids in Need

# SORES ON HIS LEGS, DIRT ON HIS FACE

You've probably seen those ads, the ones with the sad-eyed little kid standing in the middle of an unpaved street. He's got on a pair of shorts, and he's not wearing any shirt. There are sores on his legs and dirt on his face. He lives some place in Africa or Southeast Asia or South America. He doesn't go to school. He doesn't go to the doctor. He doesn't get enough to eat. The ad says all it takes to feed, clothe, educate, and keep him healthy is $20 a month.

Twenty bucks a month! That's $240 a year, a lot of money to a kid.

## What You Can Do

Pool your resources. Get together with a group of other kids. If ten of you agree to adopt a child for a year, then you each have to pay only $24 a year or $2 a month. Adopting a kid can be a Sunday School, troop, or class project. One person in your group can collect the money. Another can be the correspondent (letter writer). That's another important part of the deal; you're supposed to write letters to the kid you've adopted and send pictures. And he or she, in turn, is supposed to write back and send pictures to you. Your group and the child you adopt can learn a lot about each other and each other's countries. This adoption business could turn out to be very interesting!

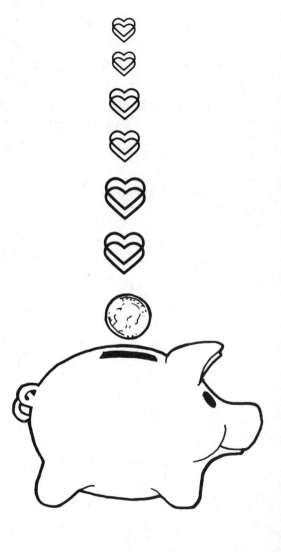

For information on how to adopt a kid, contact:

Save the Children, 54 Wilton Road, P.O. Box 940, Westport, CT 06881.
Telephone: (800) 243-5075.

Children's Aid International, 1420 Third Avenue, San Diego, CA 92101.
Telephone: (800) 842-2810.

Christian Children's Fund, 2821 Emery Wood Parkway, P.O. Box 26511,
Richmond, VA 23261. Telephone: (800) 776-6767.

Pearl S. Buck Foundation, Box 181, Perkasie, PA 18944. Telephone: (800)
220-2825.

Plan International USA, 155 Plan Way, Warwick, RI 02886. Telephone: (800)
556-7918.

*It's terrible but true*—40,000 of the world's children die every day for lack of basic health care and medicine.

# UP A CREEK

Remember that time in third grade when you were having trouble with math? You just didn't get it.

Your mom or dad may have pulled you out of that one. For weeks and weeks, they worked with you after school until you finally understood how to do the problems.

But what if your parents didn't have the time? Or didn't understand the new math? It happens to a lot of boys and girls. Where are those kids? Up a creek?

Not if you're willing to help. Here's some suggestions.

## What You Can Do

Offer to help other kids learn how to do things they're having trouble with in school. Become a tutor. You can be any age—a 1st grader helping a kindergartener or another 1st grader—a 6th grader helping someone in your own class or younger. If there's no tutoring program in your school, ask your teacher about starting one. Or ask your parent, Scout or Camp Fire leader to look into after-school tutoring programs that already exist. The YWCA/YMCA is a good place to look. Get involved! If the world is going to work when you grow up, there have to be educated people to run it. It's up to you to help them learn.

*Keep in mind: You don't have to be a genius to tutor other kids. In fact, you might even be having trouble with learning yourself.*

# THE BIRTHDAY CLUB

Every kid should have toys. Lots of toys. But for many kids living in homeless shelters, homes for abused children, and orphanages, toys are a pretty rare thing.

## What You Can Do

Start a Birthday Club. This is something for a group to do. First, you have to find the kids you want to give birthday gifts to. You can contact shelters, children's centers, or orphanages. Or call one of the national clearing houses listed on page 94 to find out about organizations for needy kids in your town. What you do is select one place and ask the person in charge to let you know when kids have their birthday.

Then have your class or club make or buy a gift and send it to each kid on their birthday. Make sure you find out the name and age of the kid; that helps make the toy more personal. And don't forget to include a birthday card. Homemade ones are really nice.

To pay for the presents you'll be sending all year long, you will need money. You can raise the money through dues, maybe a quarter a month is all you will need, or you can raise money as a group. See page 107 for how to raise money.

toys
-4-
Maple
shelter

*Keep in mind: It doesn't take a lot of money to give a kid a birthday present. Small toys like yo-yos or a coloring book and crayons are just as cherished as more expensive ones.*

## More Great Ideas

• If you know a needy family in your town, *your family* can form a Birthday Club all on its own.

• Outgrown your bike or skateboard? Don't throw it away. Give it to an orphanage or a kids' shelter. Ask your friends to do the same.

• Find out what your school does with its used sports equipment. The softball or soccer team might not be able to play in tournaments with a really old ball, but a bunch of kids who are playing for fun just might love to have it.

• Have a toy drive. Here's how you do it:

   1. Once you've found a place to give the toys to, be sure to ask somebody in charge what kinds of toys they think are needed.
   Kids living in a homeless shelter might really like a bicycle, but until they have a place to keep it, it's not practical. Smaller items—dolls, stuffed animals, cards, and board games—are easier for them to keep with them.
   Kids living in an orphanages might be able to make use of sports equipment like baseballs, bats, and gloves or volleyballs. Arts-and-crafts supplies are also welcome.

2. Make posters for your school, church, or community center advertising where to bring the toys and what kind of toys are needed. Sometimes people, especially adults, need some help in imagining the kind of toys kids would want. Here's some ideas for things you can collect: stuffed animals and dolls, puppets, trucks, building blocks, board games, frisbees, balls, roller skates. Don't forget the simple things like jacks, yo-yos, paper dolls, coloring books, crayons, and finger paints.

3. Why not ask toy stores for donations? Go in person; ask to speak to the manager and be sure to explain exactly who you are collecting the toys for. Be ready to give them the name and telephone number of an adult they can call, or bring an adult with you.

4. Christmas is always a good time for a toy drive. If you're collecting presents for Christmas, you will want to wrap them. Label the box with the kind of toy inside and the age of the kid who would enjoy it. That way the people who are handing them out can make sure each kid gets something right for them.

*Keep in mind: You can also make toys. Ask an art teacher or your parent to help you make puppets.*

# IT'S LONELY

Have you ever heard the term latchkey kids? Maybe you're one yourself. It means that when you go home after school, there's no adult there. You're on your own. Totally.

"Hey, that's great!" says the kid who goes home to a parent every day. "Nobody to boss me around, tell me what to do. Just what I always wanted."

It *isn't* great. Sometimes it's lonely. And it's a lot of responsibility. It's up to you to check out what the unfamiliar sounds are, and make sure that your little brother stays out of trouble. Then the doorbell rings. You don't know who's there. Should you answer it? And what do you do in an emergency? There's a lot to know when you're by yourself.

## What You Can Do

Start an "Afterschool Hotline" for latchkey kids. The **Campfire Girls and Boys of America** have such a program. Older members take regular weekly turns as phone counsellors. They talk to elementary school kids who call in about all sorts of things, from fears to general conversation about sports and music.

**For information on how to start a hotline for latchkey kids, contact Camp Fire, Inc., 4601 Madison Avenue, Kansas City, MO 64112-1278. Telephone: (816) 756-1950.**

## More Great Ideas

• Is one of your friends a latchkey kid? Ask your mom if you can invite him or her to your house one day a week. Then ask your friend to join your Scout troop or after-school service club. If there's a YWCA/YMCA nearby, find out if there are after-school programs the two of you can join.

• Join the Red Cross BATmen team. That's a group of older boys and girls who are instructors in Basic Aid Training (BAT), a six-session course in basic home-survival skills. The BAT course teaches kids who are left in charge of the house what to do in case of emergency.

**For information on the BAT program, contact your local chapter of the American National Red Cross or their headquarters at 18th and D Streets, NW, Washington, D.C. 20006. Telephone: (202) 737-8300.**

### SUCCESS STORY

After taking the BAT course, a nine year old was able to save his grandfather's life after his grandfather collapsed with a heart attack. Obviously, the BAT course can help adults as well as kids.

# CAMP HOME-AWAY-FROM-HOME

Summer. Your favorite time of year. Swimming, baseball, backyard cookouts. Maybe even a couple of weeks at camp.

But what if there's no backyard? No pool or lake to swim in? No money for camp? Not even a vacant lot to play in? That's the way it is for a lot of city kids. For them, summer is one long, hot bore.

The **Fresh Air Fund** is doing something about this. Since 1877, when a small group of kids from the poorer sections of New York City visited host families on farms in Sherman, Pennsylvania, the Fund has provided more than 1.6 million underprivleged New York kids with free vacations.

## What You Can Do

Invite a city kid to visit in your home. You don't have to live on a farm to do this. Even a suburb will do. You don't have to live close to New York City, either. The Fresh Air Fund sends kids to thirteen Eastern states and Canada for a two- week vacation. The Fund pays their transportation and insurance expenses. All you have to do is see that they have a good time. And with swimming, games, and backyard cookouts, that shouldn't be hard to do.

**For information about how to turn your home into a city kid's camp, contact the Fresh Air Fund,**

**1040 Avenue of the Americas**
**New York, NY   10018**
**Telephone: (800)367-0003.**

# SAFETY FIRST

You may not think of safety as a need, but it is. Bike safety, particularly. One 4-H club knew all about the importance of bike safety. They formed Bike Patrols in conjunction with the State Department of Public Safety and local police departments. They issued citations to bikers who violated bike safety rules and taught other kids how to ride safely.

A McDonald's restaurant in Paragould, Arkansas, set up a bike-safety program also. Kids on bikes paraded down Main Street, and prizes were awarded for the best-decorated ones. Members of the local police force were on hand and afterwards bike safety was discussed and demonstrated.

**If you'd like to start a similar program in your town, contact McDonald's of Paragould Arkansas, One Medical Drive, Paragould, AK 77450. Telephone: (501) 236-3715.**

## What You Can Do

Stage an after-school Bike Rodeo where you demonstrate safe biking and teach everyone about the importance of wearing bike helmets. To help make the rodeo fun, show others how you can decorate helmets with stickers, neon decals, and paint.

Ask a local bike shop to participate. Or ask them for donations. You could even hold a raffle to give away a new bike as a prize and use the money you've earned for your bike safety efforts. (For how to hold a raffle, see page 109.)

Be sure you get information on your town or state's bicycle "laws" to give away at the rodeo. Contact the police department in your town and ask them if they have a book or pamphlet on bike safety and rules of the road. If they don't, you're going to have to make one yourself. Ask your teacher or adult advisor if they can arrange for an officer to come to your class or club. Make your own booklet based on the things he or she tells you. Be sure to have an adult advisor check it carefully for errors and ask the police officer to look it over, too. Then make enough copies to give to everyone at the rodeo.

## More Great Ideas

• There are other safety problems that kids can help with. Traffic safety is one. Are there plenty of traffic lights on the streets you cross every day? Is there a particularly dangerous intersection near your school? If there is, call attention to the problem.

Tell your parents and tell your teachers. Write letters to the newspaper, to the police department, to the school board. Ask your parents or teacher to find out the name of the elected official who is responsible—and write to him or her. Write the Mayor—even if you live in a big city. Keeping people safe is part of the Mayor's job.

Most towns and cities have telephone numbers listed under "Complaints" in the City Government Office section (in the white or blue pages). Some have a separate number for "Roads" or "Traffic Lights." If you call in with a complaint, they have to investigate the problem.

• Safe places to play is another big problem. Do the kids in your neighborhood have a playground? Or do they have to play in the streets? Which leads to my next...

# SUCCESS STORY

James Ale lives in Davie, Florida. James was eight years old when he watched a car nearly hit a friend playing in the street. James decided that it was up to him to see that the kids in his town had a safe place to play. What James had in mind was a town playground.

James got himself a briefcase and became a familiar sight around Davie. He spent hours every week writing letters and making phone calls to town officials. He talked to reporters. He didn't get discouraged by how long it was taking, he just kept at it.

Finally, the town had to give James what he wanted. Two years after he began working for a playground, James got it.

Even the mayor showed up at the playground opening. He said, "James Ale could teach a lot of adults I know about lobbying local government."

*Keep in mind: Safety is really important when it comes to guns. You know that you should never, ever touch a gun. They're pretty tricky things and it might go off. You or somebody you care about could get seriously hurt—even killed. Make the world a safer place; if a kid in your school or neighborhood brags about having a gun, take it seriously. Tell your parents or your teacher immediately. You really could be saving someone's life.*

# GET APPOINTED

You must realize by now that when it comes to helping kids in need, you've got a lot to offer. Maybe you've even begun to do something about it, like getting your scout troop to adopt the kids in a homeless shelter, or becoming involved in a tutoring program, or holding a toy drive.

You may also have begun to see that adults don't always have all the answers. And maybe that's because grownups' heads are so high in the air that they miss what's going on at ground level. But your head is a lot closer to the ground. You see things the grownups may miss. Make your viewpoint heard.

## What You Can Do

Get appointed to the school board, the PTA board, the crime commission, the parks and recreation board, the youth commission, or the city council. A lot of these organizations allow kids to participate. And if some of them don't, you might be able to change that and convince the powers-that-be that when it comes to solving problems—particularly kids' problems—kids themselves have a lot to offer.

*Keep in mind: It's much easier to get appointed to committees if you don't ask for a vote. Not having a vote doesn't mean that you don't have any power. All you really need is to make yourself heard. If your ideas are carefully thought out and well presented, adults will listen to them.*

Looking for information on how to go about getting appointed to power boards? Read *The Kids Guide to Social Action*, by Barbara A. Lewis, Free Spirit Publishing.

The National Network of Youth Advisory Boards helps kids plan and evaluate youth programs. It also can help you write proposals for your ideas for programs. If you're thinking of becoming an advocate, getting appointed, or starting your own program this can be a lot of help. Contact the National Network of Youth Advisory Boards at P.O. Box 402036, Ocean View Branch, Miami Beach, FL 33140. Telephone: (305) 532-2607.

## SUCCESS STORY

Teddy Andrews was eight when he got himself named to the Youth Commission in Berkeley, California. Teddy decided that the Youth Commission (an organization that until Teddy came aboard hadn't done much) was the perfect vehicle to help needy kids.

Teddy really shook up the Youth Commission. He came up with the idea of a citywide Wish List for kids. Teddy asked nonprofit organizations and city agencies serving children to draw up lists of their needs and wants. Then Teddy led the Youth Commissioners in asking for donations from local businesses to fill those needs. Now that his Wish List is well on its way to success, Teddy is investigating unsafe playgrounds.

# HELPING THE PLANET AND ANIMALS

# SNOW LEOPARDS DON'T COME CHEAP

Many animals face the same dangers humans do; overcrowding, hunger, pollution. Certain animals, like certain humans, are even the victims of prejudice. People think they're mean and no good. Therefore they don't care about them, and sometimes even kill them. Or they kill them because they want their hides for coats or their horns for jewelry.

*Important Fact*: Nearly all of Africa's elephants will be gone in 20 years if the present rate of killing continues.

The black rhinoceros, elephant, humpback whale, mountain gorilla, snow leopard, mountain lion, and crocodile are now endangered species and face the threat of extinction. (Extinct means vanished, vamoosed, never coming back.)

# What You Can Do

Sponsor a species! Lots of kids' classes and clubs do this. The New York Zoological Society has a program to save over 50 vanishing species. When a species is disappearing, it's very important that the animals that remain get a chance to have babies. One of the things the Sponsor-a-Species program does is pay for breeding programs.

It also helps to feed them and to take care of them. Supporting an animal for a year can cost as little as $50 for some animals and as much as $2,000 for a snow leopard.

In the early 1900s, the American bison (that's a buffalo) was in serious danger of becoming extinct. The New York Zoological Society helped save the buffalo. Now they live on reserves in several states where they can eat, play, and have babies.

**For more information, contact Sponsor-a-Species, The New York Zoological Society, Bronx, NY 10460. Telephone: (212) 220-5100.**

*Important fact*: According to The Nature Conservancy—another great organization dedicated to saving endangered animals—our planet is now losing up to three species a day.

**You can get a complete list of endangered and threatened species from the Publications Unit, U.S. Fish and Wildlife Service, Washington, D.C. 20240.**

# IT HAPPENS HERE, TOO

Maybe when you think of endangered animals, you think of things like elephants and tigers in faraway places like Africa. But there are many animals in the United States that are in danger. Prairie dogs, gray wolves, bald eagles, brown pelicans, grizzly bears, and Florida panthers are endangered species living right here in America.

## What You Can Do

Find out if there are any endangered species in your neck of the woods. Write to **Defenders of Wildlife, World Wildlife Fund, The National Wildlife Federation**, and they'll tell you. (Addresses are listed below.)

You wrote and found out that there *are* endangered species where you live. Study the problem—make it a club or class project.

1. Go to the library and find out all that you can about the animal and its habitat. Important: Find out why it's becoming extinct. If the library doesn't have the information you need, don't worry, you can still find out.

2. Call your local zoo or a local chapter of the Zoological Society. Explain that you need to speak to somebody about endangered species and tell them which animal you're studying.

3. Contact groups (the same ones you wrote to) involved in saving the endangered animal and ask them if they have any more information or if they can refer you to somebody who does.

Now, do something about it:

1. An endangered animal in your state is news! Send a letter to the editor of your local newspaper or write an article for the local or school newspaper.

2. Find out if there's a Wildlife Sanctuary or Survival Center close by. Visit, call, or write and ask them what they are doing about the problem. Then ask them how you can help.

3. Help raise money for the organizations fighting to save the animal.

4. Call attention to the problem in your school and town; if you can help get others concerned then there will be a lot more people fighting to save endangered animals.

5. Send letters to your elected officials, your mayor, your congressperson, your town council. To write your state's senator or congressperson, address the letter to: Congressperson, House Office Building, Washington, D.C. 20515. Senator, Senate Office Building, Washington, D.C. 20510. Ask your parent or teacher to help you get the names and addresses of other local officials. Write letters asking them what they are going to do about it? Give them suggestions.
**The Center for Marine Conservation** knows how effective letter writing can be. This group works to protect marine mammals and fisheries against pollution. Kids can become involved in their "Seagrass" program. Seagrass organizes letter writing campaigns to help convince politicians to pay attention to marine life. It's a good way to learn about this letter writing business.

**Write to The Center for Marine Conservation, Suite 500, 1725 De Sales Street, NW, Washington, D.C. 20036. Telephone: (202) 429- 5609.**

Okay, what if you wrote and found out that there aren't any endangered species in your area. You're off the hook, right? Wrong. There are still plenty of things you can do.

• Help other animals survive. Get in touch with a Wild Life Refuge Center. These places take in sick or wounded animals, make them better, then release them into the wild again. For how to find one, check out the telephone book. (By now, you should be good at this.) Offer to feed the animals, clean out pens, raise the money necessary to keep the place going.

• You can help save endangered animals in other parts of the country or world. Attack the problem the same way you would if it existed in your own backyard. Find out what's causing it, then contact some of the organizations listed below that are doing something about it. Raise money—ask them how you can help.

**Great organizations fighting to save endangered animals:**

**Defenders of Wildlife, Inc., 1244 19th Street, NW, Washington, D.C. 20036. Telephone: (202) 659-9510.**

**The Nature Conservancy, 1815 North Lynn Street, Arlington, VA 22209. Telephone: (703) 841-5300.**

**World Wildlife Fund, 1250 24th Street, Suite 500, Washington, D.C. 20037. Telephone: (202) 293-4800.**

**National Wildlife Federation, 1400 16th Street, NW, Washington, D.C. 20036. Telephone: (202) 797-6800.**

# NO PLACE TO GO

One of the reasons why animals are in danger is because their homes are in danger. Pollution is destroying the places where they live. Cities, towns, farms, and factories are being built on top of their homes.

Ducks that live in the South can't pack up and move to Alaska where there's plenty of space. They wouldn't survive in the cold.

## What You Can Do

• In America, the wetlands, places where water and land meet, are in serious danger. They're disappearing and the many bird and fish species that live there are in real trouble.

**Ducks Unlimited** works to protect waterfowl (ducks and other birds) and their homes—the wetlands. This national conservation organization has chapters in every state. A kids' class or group can work on a local wetland cleanup project or a project to build wooden duck houses and clean and prepare them before each nesting season. The kids' group of Ducks Unlimited is called "Greenwing."

For $5 you get membership in Ducks Unlimited and kids up to age 11 receive their kids' magazine, *Puddler*. Kids age 11 to 17 receive the regular *Ducks Unlimited* magazine. See if there's a chapter near you or contact their national headquarters: Ducks Unlimited, One Waterfowl Way, Long Grove, IL 60047-9153. Telephone: (708)-438-4300

Contact the National Audubon Society for more information on saving the wetlands. See if there's a local chapter near you or write to their national headquarters: National Audubon Society, 950 Third Avenue, New York, NY 10012. Telephone: (212) 832-3200.

• When you save the rain forest, you're saving not just the trees but the animals who live in it as well. Over half the world's plant and animal species are in the rain forest. Read more about saving the rain forests on page 78.

• Create a wildlife habitat in your community, a place where animals are safe and like to hang out. This is a popular project of the **National Association of Keystone Clubs**. You can do this in a rural area or a suburb. You can even do it in the middle of a city.

For information on becoming part of The National Association of Keystone Clubs' effort to build Backyard Wildlife Habitats, contact Boys and Girls Clubs of America, 771 First Avenue, New York, NY 10017. Telephone: (212) 351-5900.

For more information on how to start your own wildlife habitat, write: National Wildlife Federation, Backyard Wildlife Program, 1400 16th Street, NW, Washington, D.C. 20036. Telephone: (202) 797-6800.

# PETS NEED FRIENDS, TOO

"Wild" animals aren't the only ones that face danger. Cats, dogs, horses, rabbits—you name them, lots of pets end up abandoned by their owners. Owners don't always want to give them up, but sometimes they can no longer afford to take care of them.

## What You Can Do

• Volunteer at an animal shelter. Help clean up, play with the animals, or do whatever's needed to make the shelter a nicer "temporary" home for the animals.

• Become a foster parent. Some shelters have temporary foster care programs. You take care of a pet until they can find a permanent home for it. It's a great way to help out.

• Instead of buying your pet from a fancy shop, get it from an animal shelter. Or look at the bulletin board at supermarkets or community centers.

• Play matchmaker. If you know somebody who has to give up their pet, try to help them find a nice new home for it. Or call your local chapter of the **Humane Society** and ask if they can refer you to a shelter that doesn't destroy the pet if the shelter can't find a home for it right away.

• Report acts of animal abuse in your community to organizations like the **American Society for the Prevention of Cruelty to Animals** or your local Animal Welfare Office.

## Another Great Idea

The **Fund for Animals** does a lot of things for animals. They help get wild animals on the endangered list and they also have two shelters for neglected or abused animals. One is a ranch in Texas called Black Beauty Ranch. And it's not just for horses; they even have elephants and chimps! The other is in California and it has lots of cats and dogs and other small pets. You or your group can donate money to help feed and care for these animals.

**For more information about their activities, write or call: The Fund for Animals, Inc., 200 West 57th Street, Suite 508, New York, NY 10019. Telephone: (212) 246-2096.**

*Keep in mind: There's something very simple you can do for the animals in your own backyard. Hang a bird-feeder. Make keeping it supplied with seeds your responsibility.*

# "LIKE BABIES, ONLY THEY DON'T CRY"

Do you like trees? Who doesn't? Without them, the world would be a desert.

But trees are in trouble. Big trouble! Forests are being cut down for roads, for farming, and, of course, to make paper. Pollution is killing a lot of others. It really could happen. The world could turn into a desert.

If trees are going to survive, they need all the help they can get. Says one kid involved in helping trees stay alive, "I'm learning that to take care of trees is like taking care of babies, only they don't cry."

Trees are more than beautiful to look at. Did you know that one mature tree consumes an average of 13 pounds of carbon dioxide per year that would otherwise pollute the atmosphere?

## What You Can Do

If you see a tree that's in trouble, try to save it. Pamper it, water it, or don't water it as the case may be. Find out what's wrong with it and how to make it better. Call up a nursery, look in a book, ask your science teacher. The Forest Service distributes several excellent free pamphlets on planting and growing healthy trees.

**Free Tree Pamphlets from the U.S. Forest Service**
Keeping Trees Healthy - # A7800430
Trees are Valuable - # A7800429
Planting a Tree - # A7800428

Write: Forest Service, U.S. Department of Agriculture, P.O. Box 2417, Washington, D.C. 20013, and include the number of the pamphlet you want.

What if you can't make that sick tree better? What if you do all you can and it dies anyway? Plant another one. Plant a bunch. Plant them in your backyard. Plant them in cities along curbs, in vacant lots, in the country, in the mountains. You can do this on your own, with friends, with your class, club, or family. Contact the organizations listed below if you need help getting started.

## More Great Ideas

• Adopt trees that are already alive. For only $35, you can buy a whole acre of tropical rain forest and make sure that it stays an acre of rain forest forever.

**Here's how you do it. There's this great organization called The Children's Rainforest. It was started by a bunch of kids. You send them $35 and they buy an acre of rain forest. Write to The Children's Rainforest, P.O. Box 936, Lewiston, ME 04240.**

*Important Fact*: Did you know that 40 percent of the Earth's oxygen comes from the rain forests in the Amazon? Yet rain forests are being burned and cut down so fast that they'll all be gone in a hundred years if nobody does anything about it. And once a rain forest is gone, that's it. It's gone forever. It will never come back.

• Redwoods, which only grow in California and southern Oregon are the world's tallest and amongst its oldest trees. Some of them are

THOUSANDS of years old. There isn't much redwood forest left and like the rainforest, it needs protection. You know what to do: Call attention to the problem.

Or you can raise money to help save the redwood trees. Save-the-Redwoods League raises money to purchase redwoods land to be added to the national, state, or local park system. Write to them at 114 Sansome Street, Room 605, San Francisco, CA 94104. Telephone: (415) 362-2352.

• For $25, you can help protect the rain forest by supporting native tribes' efforts to own the land. In the Amazon $25 has protected as many as 1,750 acres. You get a certificate of recognition stating how much rain forest you helped protect, what tribe you have helped support, and where they are located.

Contact the Rainforest Action Network, 450 Sansome Street, Suite 700, San Francisco, CA 94111. Telephone: (415) 398-2732. Tell your teacher they also have educational materials for grades K-12.

• Call attention to the problems trees are having. Join groups working to save trees. Make a lot of noise. Make posters, get your friends, classmates, and parents involved. Remember, trees don't cry, so you have to do it for them! Get help from these organizations:

**Global Releaf Program, American Forestry Association, P.O. Box 2000, Washington, D.C. 20013. Telephone: (800) 368-5748.**

**Trees for Life, Inc., 1103 Jefferson Street, Wichita, KS 67203. Telephone: (316) 263-7294.**

**National Arbor Day Foundation, 100 Arbor Avenue, Nebraska City, NE 68410. Telephone: (402) 474-5655.**

**TreePeople, 12601 Mulholland Drive, Beverly Hills, CA 90210. Telephone: (818) 753-4600.**

**Rainforest Action Network, 450 Sansome Street, Suite 700, San Francisco, CA 94111. Telephone: (415) 398-4404.**

• Recycle or use less of the products made from trees: Paper, envelopes, newspapers, paper cups, paper plates, napkins, milk cartons, are a few examples. Did you know that if you recycle a four-foot stack of newspapers you save one tree from being cut down? You do now.

## SUCCESS STORY

Andy Lipkis is a kid from Los Angeles, California. When Andy was at summer camp in the mountains outside the city, he noticed that pollution was killing the trees around the camp. Then Andy found out that pollution wasn't killing only those trees, but all over the mountains. Andy organized a group of campers to plant smog-resistant trees. The effort grew into TreePeople, a band of volunteer citizen foresters that has planted millions of trees in the Los Angeles area and around the world.

# YUCK, YUCK, AND PE-EW!

They used to call it garbage. Now it's solid waste, liquid waste, toxic waste. Toxic means poisonous. Whatever garbage is called, there's an awful lot if it. It's ugly to look at, terrible to smell, makes people sick, and sometimes even kills them.

Most of our garbage is dumped into landfills. That means it's buried in the earth. Did you know that half of the cities in the United States will run out of landfill space in the next few years. What happens then? If garbage is burned or dumped at sea it pollutes the air and ocean. More important, what are you planning to do about it?

## What You Can Do

Educate yourself: Visit a garbage dump! Yes, it may stink but how else can you really find out about this garbage problem? Ask your parents if they will take you—or get together with a club or class and organize a trip. Call first and ask if you can come and if there will be someone to show you around and answer your questions. Then ask lots of them. Ask what happens to waste once it gets there? Is it burned? Is it buried? How long does it take various items to decompose? An apple? A pair of pantyhose? A tin can?

You can use this information for your recycling projects—at home or in your classroom. One day you and your friends will be in charge of the planet—and this garbage problem isn't going to go away all by itself.

*Important facts*: Some metal cans can last 200 years and some plastic as long as 500 years. Right now plastic recycling is hard to do because there are so many different types of plastic and it's difficult to sort. Plastic soda bottles and milk containers are the easiest and they're often recycled. Plastic recycling is going to be very important in your lifetime so make sure you learn about it.

## More Great Ideas

• Here's a fascinating project. Keep track of all the solid waste your family creates in one day. Weigh it and determine how much paper, glass, metal, and plastic is used. These are the four groups of things that can all be recycled.

Decide how much of the waste isn't necessary. Were there lots of plastic bags in there? Or lots of paper that was hardly used? Take a pledge to cut out the unnecessary stuff and to reuse whatever you can.

• Recycle. You've heard it before. Over and over. You hear it because recycling is a major part of the solution to the waste problem. Find out what the recycling facilities are in your town. How? Look in the good old yellow pages. See what's listed under "Recycling," or "Environmental Agencies." Call your town or city hall.

**Write or call The Environmental Defense Fund, 275 Park Avenue South, New York, NY 10010. Telephone: (212) 505-2100. Ask for their help in locating the nearest center.**

**The National Recycling Coalition has lots of information and brochures and pamphlets on recycling issues. Write or call them at 1101 30th Street, NW, Washington, D.C. 20007. Telephone: (202) 625-6406.**

*Keep in mind: Some recycling centers don't take plastic or some kinds of metal so it's important to contact the center. They can tell you what kind of material they take and how to sort your garbage.*

• No recycling center near by? Help get one started. Get hold of a copy of *The Recycler's Handbook*. It's available at bookstores and libraries, or send $5.95 (includes postage and handling) to the EarthWorks Group, 1400 Shattuck Avenue, #25, Berkeley, CA 94709. You can do it. Kids can do just about anything they set their minds to.

• Help make recycling the law. Some states have made recycling the law, but not all. In 1992 only Florida, Washington, Oregon, New York, Pennsylvania, Rhode Island, Connecticut, New Jersey, and Maryland did. If it isn't the law in your state, write your state legislator and ask why. Organize a letter-writing campaign. The more letters they receive the harder it will be to ignore it.

• Don't just recycle, but buy things that have been made from recycled materials. Look for paper, plastic, and glass products made from recycled materials; look at the packaging of items you buy to see if they're made from recycled ingredients.

# LITTER-LY YOURS

Pick it up! Clean up after yourself! You've been hearing these things all your life. When it comes to litter, all of the above apply.

## What You Can Do

• Look around your town or neighborhood. Pick an especially dirty place—a park, a playground, the street in front of your school, a riverbank on the outskirts of town. CLEAN IT UP! Once you've got it clean, make sure it stays that way. Make regular clean-up visits. Post signs saying DO NOT LITTER. Be persistent.

• If there's a kind of litter that especially bugs you, go after that. For a girl I know, it was Styrofoam cups. She not only got her friends to pick them up, she got them to take the cups back to the fast food places where they came from. She and her friends asked the fast food places to switch to another kind of cup. They wouldn't, so she and her friends took their fight to the town council, and the town council banned the cups.

• Here's a great way to clean things up and raise money at the same time. Hold a Litter-thon. Get a group of kids together and a large canvas bag for each of them. Pick an area that needs to be cleaned up—maybe a park—and ask adults to sponsor you for every sack of litter you collect. Remember, you'll need some jumbo garbage bags to hold all the litter you've collected. (Find some that were made from recycled material or are biodegradable.) Use the money you've raised to help environmental organizations—or to purchase some more of that rain forest! Pretty soon a lot of that forest is going to belong to kids.

• Make other people's litter your responsibility. Pick up the stuff you see on the sidewalk. Throw it in a nearby trash can.

• The next time you go to a beach or other public recreational area, take along a big canvas bag and spend a few minutes filling it with trash.

For more information on litter, write or call Keep America Beautiful, Mill River Plaza, 9 West Broad Street, Stamford, CT 06902. Telephone: (203) 323-8987. There are over 400 local chapters so check your phone book first. They help groups clean up litter and stop litter before it happens with recycling projects. They also have helpful information written for kids on litter and recycling. Tell your teacher that they have curriculum materials for grades K - 12.

*Keep in mind: It's that "R" word again. Recycling helps keep cans and bottles off the street. You can help by launching a can or bottle drive. (This is a great way to raise money for all sorts of worthy causes, too.)*

## How to Start a School-wide Can and Bottle Drive

1. First you need to find a redemption center or local bottler to take your cans and bottles. Check the yellow pages. Ask your teacher or an adult to help you. Write or call the recycling groups listed at the back of the book for help.

The bottler or redemption center will tell you what kinds of materials they can take and how you should sort them. And they will give you money for each bottle and can you bring in.

2. Before you start, get organized. You'll need a president to recruit volunteers, a treasurer to keep track of all the money you raise, a press co-ordinator to take charge of posters, a teacher or other school "official" to help you work with the redemption center and school administration, and drivers to transport the cans and bottles.

3. You need to figure out how the cans and bottles will be moved from collection centers to the redemption center. Some redemption centers will pick them up, but most will expect you to bring them to them. You'll have to sign up some parents or teachers to volunteer their cars and time.

4. Next you need to create collection centers. You'll need at least one large garbage can at each location. Probably two - one for glass and/or plastic bottles and one for cans. Make sure you put some near the lunchroom! If your school is big you'll want more than one location.

Someone has to check the collection centers daily and when they're full move the contents into a bigger storage space, a basement, janitor's supply room, or any space where trash is usually kept.

5. You need to advertise. Make posters announcing your plans and place them all over the school. Make sure you include what you're raising the money for. If you plan to keep the drive going for a while make sure you update the posters to tell how much money you've raised so far.

# AND YOU THOUGHT IT WAS FREE?

You've probably heard the expression, "Free as the air you breathe."

I've got news for you. Air that's fit to breathe *isn't* free anymore. We all have to pay for it—with dollars, with ideas, and most of all, with vigilance.

What's vigilance? Vigilance, says my dictionary, is watchfulness.

When it comes to the quality of the air we breathe, you can't get much more vigilant than **Kids Against Pollution (KAP)**. KAP began with a group of 5th graders in Closter, New Jersey. Now there are over 1,000 chapters of KAP around the country and in five foreign countries.

Concerned about air pollution, KAP studied what causes it. One of the biggest causes, they learned, is CFCs or chlorofluorocarbons. CFCs are tiny particles released into the atmosphere when polystyrene, (the stuff used to make Styrofoam cups), is cracked, crushed, or thrown away.

The kids from Closter wrote to schools in every county of their state alerting them to the hazards posed to the air by polystyrene. They also sent material about KAP and asked other classes to join them in the fight against CFCs. They held press conferences and they gave speeches, not just before other kids but before grownups. Along the way, some of them got pretty famous. It's funny—though most of them were sort of shy at first, they didn't mind being famous at all. In fact, they kind of like it.

But fame isn't the only thing KAP got. They got their school board to ban polystyrene in their school district. Then they got the town council to ban the stuff. They also got to go to Washington, D.C. where they testified before the Environmental Protection Agency.

Still, KAP knows that the fight for clean air has just begun. And even when it's won, it's never really over. If it's going to stay clean, vigilance is the price we'll all have to pay.

**If you'd like to join a KAP group or know more about how to fight air pollution, contact KAP, Tenakill School, 275 High Street, Closter, NJ 07624. Telephone: (201) 768-1332.**

*Keep in mind: Forming your own organization might sound like a pretty tough thing to do. Just how do you hold a press conference anyway? Although your parents and teachers can probably help you figure this out, there are several organizations that can help kids groups get big projects started. See pages* 95-97.

# STAMP OUT WATER ABUSE

Water, water, everywhere and not a drop to drink, or swim in. It could happen. People abuse water. They waste it, take it for granted, dump all kinds of bad stuff into it.

A 13-year-old girl I know discovered this the hard way. Katie Whalen is her name. One day Katie discovered that a Vermont river she had been swimming in all her life was filled with raw sewage. It made Katie furious. "This has got to stop," she said.

And Katie stopped it. It wasn't easy, and she didn't do it all by herself. She had to get a lot of other people to help her. Actually, she had to start her own environmental group. She made a lot of noise, and some people said she made a nuisance of herself, but she got it done. And even now that the river is clean and swimmable again, Katie and her group can't afford to sit back and relax. The truth is, they're going to have to keep an eye on it for the rest of their lives. Because if the river became polluted once, it could happen again.

If you are concerned about a river or other body of water near your home, here's...

## What You Can Do

Make what happens to it your responsibility. Adopt a river, a pond, a lake, an ocean. I suppose you could even adopt an irrigation ditch!

Have your club or class study the effect of raw sewage, chemicals, and other pollutants on water life. To do this your first stop is the library, then write to the environmental groups listed below and ask them to send you information.

Find out if anything bad is happening to YOUR river, YOUR pond, YOUR lake, YOUR ocean. How? One way to do this is to visit. Look at that stream or ocean carefully. Look for:

- Dead fish floating in the water.
- Really big metal cans in or near the water.
- Dead birds covered in oil on the beach.
- Patches of purple sludge in the water.
- An unusual amount of garbage: cans, papers, bottles, etc.

If you see anything like this—or anything else that looks wrong—get an adult to come and make an inspection with you. See if you can figure out what's happening.

**Contact the National Wildlife Federation. They can help you recognize the symptoms of environmental abuse. Write them at 1400 16th Street, NW, Washington, D.C. 20036. Telephone: (202) 797-6800.**

Be sure to discuss the problem with your parents and teacher. They can help you make sure you have all your facts right, so you can COMPLAIN. Look in the white or blue pages of your phone book under "City Government Offices" then look under "Environmental Protection," or "Environmental Control Board." They probably have a telephone number listed for "Complaints." It's a very good place to start.

The Environmental Protection Agency (EPA) is a government agency that will take your complaints about air and water pollution. Many of the ten regional offices have 800-numbers so the call is free. Or you can contact the Office of the Ombudsman, Room 2111, Mail-Code OS-130, U.S. Environmental Protection Agency, 401 M Street, SW, Washington, D.C. 20460. Telephone: (202) 475-9361. It's their job to protect the environment. Help them do it by letting them know if something bad is happening.

The Environmental Protection Agency is concerned about ANY kind of pollution—keep your eyes open for problems with air pollution, too.

If something is being dumped into your water and you know who is doing the dumping, write them letters and ask them to stop it. By now, of course, you realize you are probably going to have to ask more than once. You may have to ask over and over and over again. You may even have to write to newspapers, hold press conferences, go before legislative bodies and ask them to pass laws to protect your body of water. But you won't have to do this all by yourself. There are plenty of groups that can help you.

**Contact environmental groups working for clean water:**

**Citizens Clearing House for Hazardous Waste, P.O. Box 6806, Falls Church, VA 22040. Telephone: (703) 276-7070.**

**Adopt-a-Stream Foundation, P.O. Box 5558, Everett, WA 98206. Telephone: (206) 388-3487.**

**The American Oceans Campaign, 725 Arizona Avenue, Suite 102, Santa Monica, CA 90401. Telephone: (310) 576-6162.**

**Greenpeace USA, 1436 U Street, NW, Washington, D.C. 20009. Telephone: (202) 462-1177.**

The key to saving the earth in your own community is research. But research isn't hard to do and it can be a lot of fun. There are some great environmental organizations that help you become aware of problems and figure out ways to solve them. Keep reading....

# EARTH DAY IS EVERY DAY

Wouldn't it be nice to help others learn about the importance of protecting our environment. Funny thing is, you can!

## What You Can Do

• Tell your teacher about KIND News (Kids in Nature's Defense). It's a newspaper that teaches kindness, respect, and responsibility to animals and the environment. For $25 every kid in your class can get a copy each month during the school year.

**Order from NAHEE (National Association for Humane and Environmental Education), 67 Salem Road, East Haddam, CT 06423. Telephone: (203) 434-8666.**

• Audubon Adventures is an education program for grades three to six. It includes 32 copies of a bimonthly newspaper for kids and a Leader's Guide for the teacher.

**Order from your local Audubon chapter or Audubon Adventures, National Audubon Society, 613 Riversville Road, Greenwich, CT 06831. Telephone: (203) 869-5272.**

Teens aren't the only ones who can be green. Earth Day is celebrated on April 22nd. Make it a plan to become EARTH SMART by the next Earth Day. Then help celebrate by sharing your knowledge with your friends and family.

# GETTING STARTED

# FINDING A VOLUNTEER GROUP IN YOUR COMMUNITY

If you're having trouble finding a place where you can volunteer in your town, these nation-wide organizations will help you find them.

Also, if you want to collect food, clothing, toys, etc., and aren't sure whom to give them to, the local chapters of these groups may be able to help you find the right people.

**Points of Light Foundation** has over 400 branches in the U.S. If you call their toll-free number, they will send you a very helpful book called a "fulfillment booklet." It lists lots of names and numbers of volunteer organizations in your area. Even if you already know what you want to do and where you can do it, this is an excellent booklet to have. You can share it with others who want to make a difference.

**Call: Points of Light Foundation, Telephone: (800) 879-5400.**

**Volunteers of America** operates its own programs for the homeless, elderly, developmentally disabled, etc., across the country. They suggest that you first call your local chapter of Volunteers of America (it should be listed in the phone book) and tell them the kind of volunteer work you want to do; they will try to match you up with a program. If they don't have an existing program they will do their best to refer you to another. You can also call or write their national headquarters.

**Contact: Volunteers of America, 3813 North Causeway Boulevard, Metairie, LA 70002. Telephone: (504) 837-2652.**

**Four-One-One** is another national volunteer group that runs a variety of volunteer projects in communities. (See Super Volunteers!, page 96.) They suggest you check your phone book first to see if there's a local chapter. They, too, will refer you to volunteer groups in your community.

**Contact: Four-One-One, 7304 Beverly Street, Annandale, VA 22003. Telephone: (703) 354-6270.**

# GREAT ORGANIZATIONS THAT HELP KIDS HELP OTHERS IN THEIR TOWN

## STARSERVE

Students Taking Action and Responsibility in Service, **StarServe**, is a great organization dedicated to getting kids involved in helping their communities. It was started by Mike Love, one of the members of the band the Beach Boys, and provides teachers and students with free materials and assistance to plan community service projects in and outside the classroom. It also provides book lists for kindergarten through 12th grade on community service themes, and videos to motivate kids, teachers, and parents.

In addition, StarServe publishes a national newsletter highlighting kids' community service projects around the country.

Contact: StarServe, P.O. Box 34567, Washington, D.C. 20043. Telephone: (800) 888-8232.

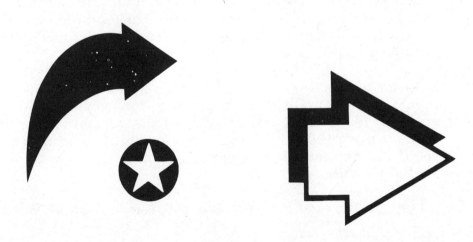

95

## SUPER VOLUNTEERS!

**Super Volunteers!**, part of the national **Four-One-One** organization works with kids age four to seventeen who belong to traditional kids' organizations like Boy and Girl Scouts, 4-H, Camp Fire, etc. Super Volunteers! aims to help kids identify problems in their communities and contribute to their solution.

Kid volunteers are expected to sign a volunteer contract, record volunteer hours, and submit program descriptions to Super Volunteers! In return, they receive T-shirts, how-to manuals, videos, and other tools for their projects. In addition, Super Volunteers! publishes the *Small World Newsletter*, edited by kids themselves. Super Volunteers is anxious to hear from you and put you to work. So what are you waiting for?

Contact: Super Volunteers!, Four-One-One, 7304 Beverly Street, Annandale, VA 22003. Telephone: (703) 354-6270.

## STANDING TALL

The **Giraffe Project** is a national organization dedicated to getting people to stick their necks out for the common good. Its Standing Tall Program is aimed at getting kids from kindergarten through high school to stick their necks out.

Standing Tall distributes a really neat program kit. The kit helps kids— in other words, *you*—identify the qualities of courage and caring that can turn you into a Giraffe, then moves on to help you identify those same qualities in yourself. Finally, the kit teaches you and your group to identify community needs and fill them through community service projects. If you'd like to stand tall in your community, ask your teacher or adult club leader to write.

Contact: The Giraffe Project, Box 759, Langley, WA 98260. Telephone: (206) 221-7989.

# CONSTITUTIONAL RIGHTS FOUNDATION (CRF)

**CRF** is another organization dedicated to getting kids to identify problems in their communities, then go to work to solve them. Most of their activities are aimed at high school kids, but a lot of their programs can be easily adapted to younger kids. One especially great program goes right to the heart of *Kids Can Help*. It's called Community Search.

Community Search teaches you and your friends how to locate places in your community where you can serve as volunteers. Places like nursing homes, libraries, hospitals, and parks that need cleaning, walls that need graffiti scrubbed off—and any other opportunities that you and your friends discover along the way. The discovery process—you and your friends literally go out and scour the neighborhood on foot—is supposed to take less than two hours. And the follow up a week later in which you and your friends zero in on the places you want to volunteer your services takes less than 30 minutes. It's an incredibly efficient process, made more so by the Community Search Kit. CRF is anxious to help you get started. So get busy and write or call.

**Contact: Constitutional Rights Foundation, 601 South Kingsley Drive, Los Angeles, CA 90005. Telephone: (213) 487- 5590.**

# USE YOUR PHONE BOOK...

The phone book is a great way to find out about needy groups and volunteer programs. Some of the headings under which volunteer groups might be listed in the yellow pages are:

Volunteer Action Centers
Voluntary Action Centers
Community Services
Social Services
Human Services
Social and Human Services
Volunteer Services

Most states have something called a Governor's Board of Volunteers. You can find the number listed under state government offices in the white or blue pages.

*Keep in mind: 800-numbers are free, but other long distance calls can cost a lot of money. Be sure to ask your parent's permission before calling.*

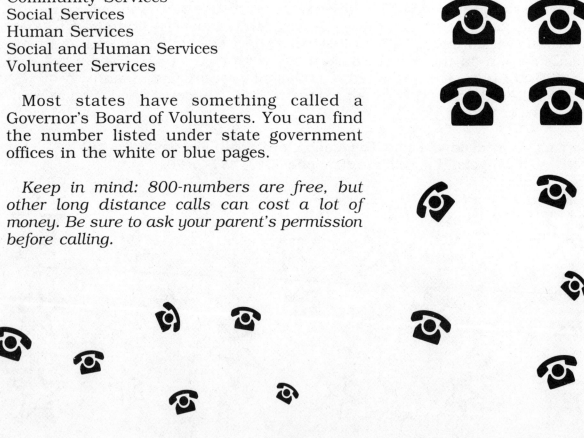

# BECOMING A PHONE PRO—OR PRACTICE MAKES PERFECT! ☎

You're almost to the end of the book now, and you're all fired-up about putting some of the ideas you've been reading about into practice. There's only one little problem. Actually, it's a big problem. It's that part about having to call up organizations and volunteer your services or ask them for information. You find that pretty intimidating. You find it downright scary, in fact.

Here's what you do. You practice.

You'll need a friend to help you. The friend can be a kid or a grownup, but in this case a grownup is probably better. You'll be the make-believe caller, the grownup will be the person who answers the phone.

But before you start practicing, write down what you want to say. Be as specific as you can. Are you looking for ideas on how you can help with a particular problem like the homeless or the elderly or the environment, or do you have a specific project or skill you'd like to offer the organization you're calling? In any case, on a piece of paper write down everything you might want to say. Start at the beginning with your name and age. Don't laugh! It's easy to forget your own name when you're nervous.

When you and the grownup are ready, sit down, keep the paper in front of you, and face the grownup across a table if possible. Both of you should make believe you've picked up a telephone. Start dialing.

Have the grownup pick up his pretend phone and say: "Coalition for the Homeless." Or: "Red Cross." Or: "Nature Conservancy." Whoever it is you're planning to call.

Now, it's your turn. Say: "My name is
_____. I'm _____ years old. I'd like
to do something to help the homeless." Or,
if you've called an organization like the Red
Cross: "I'm interested in your BAT
Program." Or if it's an organization like the
Nature Conservancy: "I want to help
endangered wildlife."

At this point, there are a number of ways
the grownup can respond, and, in fact, at
some point, he or she should play back all of
the responses listed below. That way you'll
be ready to handle any of them.

One is: "Just a minute, I'll have to put you
on hold.

WARNING: This happens a lot when you
call up volunteer organizations. So don't be
intimidated, they're not doing it to you
because you're a kid.

Another response is: "I'll have to transfer
you to _____." You'll probably be given the
name of a person or a department. (Chances
are that after you've been put on hold for a
while this will be the response.) At any rate,
when the transfer is accomplished and you
have somebody new on the line, you will have
to start all over again with your name, age,
and the information you're seeking.

The grownup can end the make-believe
conversation here if he wants. Or he can
keep on talking to you, asking more
questions. In a real life conversation, it's
hard to anticipate exactly what will happen
from here on out, you just have to go with
the flow. So relax and try to do just that.

Another response is, and this can be discouraging: "Sorry, we don't take kids."

That's your cue to say: "Could you refer me to an organization that does?"

Grownup: "Sorry, I don't know any."

You: "Well, thanks anyway."

Never lose your cool. Don't let a discouraging response throw you off balance. Learning to handle rejection is part of living. Put down that phone, and start dialing somebody else. Some volunteer organizations are still asleep to kid power. Maybe your offer to help will wake them up.

Hopefully, another response might be, "Yes, there's a group called _____."

You: "Could you give me the phone number please?" (Don't forget to keep a pencil handy so you can write down important stuff like this.)

Some organizations you call will be answered by a recording asking you to leave your name and message. This is another time not to let yourself be intimidated. Nobody really likes answering machines. Actually, I take that back. For a kid just starting out to become a phone pro, there's an advantage to talking into a machine. They don't interrupt! And since you've already written down your name, age, and what you want to say, it should be easy to say it. As long as you make your message short and snappy. So practice.

Sometimes the answering machines' message will be complicated. "Press One if you want membership information, Two if you want to talk to someone in the issues department, Three if you wish to make a donation," says a voice with enough authority in it to make you want to hang up. Would you believe it, one organization I called had nine possible digits to press? At first, it freaked me out. So this is what I did. I hung up and dialed again. Actually, I had to call three times before I could figure out which number on my phone I should punch. And even then, I was never really sure. So I just punched the number for General Information.

*Warning*: Even after you've punched the correct number, or what you hope is the correct one, don't count on getting a real live person to talk to right away. Very likely, you'll get another recording asking you to hold for a minute (it'll be more than a minute, I can almost guarantee you!) followed by the kind of music they play in elevators.

Your parents have probably told you patience is important. As you learn to become a phone pro, you'll have to practice patience a lot. But kids all over the world are doing it—and so can you.

# WRITING LETTERS

Sometimes writing a letter is easier than making a phone call. And many organizations don't have enough people to answer phones. Writing a letter is not hard. The trick is to be as specific as possible about what you want.

• When you're asking for information, also ask if they can refer you to another organization if they don't have the information you need.

• Give information about yourself: your age, where you live, and the kinds of things you would be interested in doing. For example, "I'd be interested in visiting your nursing home once a week," or "I'd like to help raise money and collect other things that people in your shelter need."

• If you're writing as a part of a group remember to say so. Say, "My girl scout troop would like to start..." or "My third grade class would like to help clean up the lake nearby."

• Most adults are worried that kids might not have their parents' permission to do things. After you've asked your parents permission, include this in your letter. For instance, you could say, "My father will bring me to the nursing home once a week," or, "I've talked about this with my parents, and we agree that collecting clothes for the homeless would be a really great thing to do."

*Keep in mind: Make sure you put your address and full name on your letter so they can write back.*

Raising Money

# COMMON CENTS

Pennies. Everybody has them lying around. In pockets, drawers, purses. They rattle around, get in the way. What can you do with a penny nowadays? They're not worth much.

STOP! You can do something GREAT with them.

This is a great money-raising idea. In fact, it's more than great. It's brilliant!

There's this little girl that lives in New York City. She was only three but she was really worried about the homeless people she saw on the streets. So she asked her dad what she could do to help them.

They decided to collect all the pennies in the house and give them to an organization that helps the homeless. The idea caught on. Soon their friends and neighbors were collecting their pennies. Before you knew it, this little girl and her father had a full-fledged penny collecting organization on their hands. They call it Common Cents.

Here's how it works. People—they're called Harvesters—collect pennies from their neighbors and put them in plastic zip-lock bags (the company that makes the bags donates them for free). After the Harvesters have collected the money, they store the bags at home until Common Cents calls a "Field Day." That's a day when everyone brings their bags of pennies to a central place, dumps them on a counter, and rolls them in paper.

Now the pennies are ready to be transported to what is called a counting house. Sometimes the pennies are transported in Harvester's cars, sometimes there are so many pennies they have to go in armored trucks! At the counting house the pennies are counted, then sent to the banks where the money is transferred to organizations for the homeless. Common Cents hates to waste even a penny, so the counting house donates its services for free.

The result? In 1991, the first year of its existence, Common Cents collected $103,268.68 for the homeless! One New York city school raised over $30,000.

Common Cents Harvesters range in age from 4 to 84, but half of them are kids and their families.

If you'd like to start a penny collecting organization to help the homeless write to Common Cents New York Inc., 500 Eighth Avenue, Room 910, New York, NY 10018. To volunteer in New York, write or call: (212) PENNIES.

# GREAT WAYS YOU CAN RAISE MONEY

You don't have to be a grownup or even a teenager to raise money for a worthy cause. There are lots of things younger kids can do on their own, or with family and friends. But whatever you decide to do, always be sure to tell people what you are raising the money for. They're sure to be more generous if they know the money is going to a good cause.

And you have to make sure people know about your efforts. Make posters you can put up around town and at school to advertise your activity. Make sure you include all the information people will need and a phone number of somebody they can call if they have any questions.

Here are some ideas to get you started.

• **Sell things.** Set up a lemonade stand. Hold a bake sale—ask your family and friends to bake cakes and cookies (and bake some yourself)! Sell homegrown vegetables and flowers. Collect old books and sell them. Hold a tag sale—collect things people don't want anymore and sell them. Hold a toy sale—sell all the toys you and your friends don't play with anymore. Have a crafts fair—sell things you, your friends, and family have made.

• **Sell services.** Sweep walks. Rake leaves. Mow and water lawns. Weed gardens. Wash cars. Walk dogs. Baby-sit. Pet-sit. Run errands. Ask your neighbors and parents' friends if they would hire you to do these things. Or make posters to advertise your services.

• **Recycle.** Take refundable bottles and cans to a supermarket or grocery store and collect the deposits.

• **Stage a marathon.** A marathon is any task or action that takes a lot of effort and lasts a long time. You probably know about running marathons, but there are lots of other kinds, too, that are used for fund-raising. The way it works is this: If you decide to stage a Walk-a-thon or a Bike-a-thon, you ask people to promise to pay a certain amount of money (the amount is up to them—a nickel, a quarter, a dollar, whatever they want) for every mile you walk or ride your bike. For a Swim-a-thon, ask them to pay for every lap you swim; for a Dance-a-thon or a Jump-a-thon, they pay for however long you can dance or jump rope.

(Of course, you don't do any of this nonstop! You're allowed to rest whenever you get tired. And unless you're a topnotch athlete in great physical shape, you'll have to build up your stamina and strength before you actually begin whatever activity you choose.)

If you're not the athletic type, try a Read-a-thon , or a Sing-a-thon.

• **Hold a potluck supper.** Ask some people to donate food, and charge others to eat it. Hold the potluck supper at someone's house, a school gym, a church rec room. Make sure you tell the diners all about the cause you're raising money for. They might even think of some other ways to help you.

• **Hold a raffle.** Get local stores to donate "prizes" like skateboards, computer games, a camera or a 10-pound bag of jellybeans. What you do is sell tickets for a chance to win the prize. You can buy raffle tickets already made at many stationery stores. Or you can make your own. The day the winning ticket is picked you might want to set up other activities—like a carnival or a lemonade stand or a concert so you can make the day fun and earn even more money. You can raffle off just one prize or a whole lot of prizes.

• **Stage a carnival.** Charge admission, and sell lemonade and popcorn. Have lots of games for people to play—bingo, beanbag toss, a sack race, hopscotch, musical chairs, a rope-jumping contest—and give the winners prize ribbons you make yourself. Ask somebody to paint funny faces on kids with makeup. Somebody else could tell fortunes.... You get the idea—use your imagination and have fun!

Of course you're going to need lots of space for a carnival. If you don't know anyone with a really big backyard, ask your school, church, or community center if they have some space you can use.

• **Put on plays or concerts.** The best plays, of course, are the ones you or your friends write. Why not write a play that relates to the cause you're raising money for? And if you or your friends sing, dance, or play any musical instrument, pool your talents for a concert or recital. Again, charge admission and sell popcorn and lemonade.

## Last But Not Least!

Think about giving something up. Give up your birthday presents one year, for example. I know that doesn't sound like much fun. But think about it. Have a birthday party, but dedicate it to an organization that you want to give money to. Have your parents and friends make a donation of money instead of giving you presents. Or let your friends buy gifts, but tell them you are going to give them to needy kids. You'll have other birthdays, but this might be one you will remember forever.

Talk to your family about giving something up. Maybe one year the money you would spend on a big Thanksgiving dinner could go to a shelter—and you could all offer to serve dinner at the shelter.

Be creative. There are probably a lot of things you could give up if you really think about it. And I guarantee it will make you feel really good.

# HAVING THE LAST WORD

You can if you want to. Did you know that you can call the President of the United States and give him your opinion about how he's doing his job? About the environment. The homeless. Drugs. Anything you want to talk about. You won't get to speak to him directly, because he's a little too busy for that. You'll talk to someone else who'll pass your message on to him.

This is the way it's done. Twice a week, phone call reports are issued to the President, along with a few particularly well-stated comments. In this case, well-stated, means brief, and intelligent; in other words, it's another time when short and snappy does the trick.

Call: White House Comment Line, Washington, D.C. Telephone (202)456-1111.

Be prepared to be put on hold. On an average day, the White House Comment Line receives 940 calls. And when something really big is happening, the number swells to 4000. If you call in the early morning, it's less likely to be busy.

# DIRECTORY OF ORGANIZATIONS

Addresses and telephone numbers listed are for the central office or national headquarters of each organization. Check your phone book first to see if there's a local chapter near you.

## JUST FOR KIDS—SOME GREAT KIDS' GROUPS YOU OR YOUR GROUP CAN JOIN OR CONTACT FOR INFORMATION

**Boy Scouts of America**, 1325 West Walnut Hill Lane, P.O. Box 152079, Irving, TX 75015-2079. Telephone: (214) 580-2000.

**Boys Club of America**, 771 First Avenue, New York, NY 10017. Telephone: (212) 351-5900.

**Camp Fire Boys and Girls, Inc.**, 4601 Madison Avenue, Kansas City, MO 64112-1278. Telephone: (816) 756-1950.

**Girl Scouts of the U.S.A.** 830 Third Avenue, New York, NY 10022. Telephone: (212) 940-7500.

**Girls Clubs of America**, 30 East 33rd Street, New York, NY 10016. Telephone: (212) 689-3700.

**Greenwing**, (see **Ducks Unlimited**, page 121).

**Keystone Clubs, National Association of**, (part of **Boys and Girls Clubs of America**), 771 First Avenue, New York, NY 10017. Telephone: (212) 351-5900.

**Kids Against Crime (KAC)**, P.O. Box 22004, San Bernadino, CA 92406. Telephone: (714) 882-1344. Operates a toll-free hotline for kids who are victims of crime. Also fights child abuse.

**Kids Against Pollution (KAP)**, Tenakill School, 275 High Street, Closter, NJ 07624. Telephone: (201) 768-1332. Fights pollution and other environmental problems.

**Kids For Saving Earth**, P.O. Box 47247, Plymouth, MN 55447- 0247. Telephone: (612) 525-0002. Fights environmental problems.

**National Network of Youth Advisory Boards**, P.O. Box 402036, Ocean View Branch, Miami Beach, FL 33140. Telephone: (305) 532- 2607.

**StarServe**, P.O. Box 34567, Washington, D.C. 20043. Telephone: (800) 888-8232. Community service projects for kids.

**Students Against Drunk Driving (SADD)**, P.O. Box 800, Marlboro, MA 01752. Telephone: (508) 481-3568. Speaks out and educates kids about the dangers of driving during or after using drugs or alcohol.

**Super Volunteers!**, part of **Four-One-One**, 7304 Beverly Street, Annandale, VA 22003. Telephone: (703) 354-6270. Organizes kids classes and clubs to volunteer in the community.

**YMCA of the USA**, 101 North Wacker Drive, Chicago, IL 60606. Telephone: (312) 977-0031; (800) USA-YMCA. Runs a variety of educational, recreational, and social programs for kids and adults.

**Youth Service America**, 1319 F Street, Suite 900, NW, Washington, D.C. 20004. Telephone: (202) 783-8855. Community service projects for kids.

## SUPERGROUPS—ORGANIZATIONS THAT SERVE A WIDE VARIETY OF CAUSES

**Four-One-One**, (see Super Volunteers! above).

**Catholic Charities USA**, 191 Joralemon Street, Brooklyn, NY 11201. Telephone: (718) 596-5500. Runs a variety of programs to help the needy.

**Points of Light Foundation**. Call (800) 879-5400 for their free pamphlet of volunteer organizations in your area.

**United Way of America**, 1701 North Fairfax Street, Alexandria, VA 22314. Telephone: (703) 836-7100. Runs a variety of programs to help the needy.

**Volunteers of America**, 3813 North Causeway Boulevard, Metairie, LA 70002. Telephone: (504) 837-2652. Runs volunteer programs for the homeless, elderly, disabled, etc. in communities throughout the United States.

## SOME ORGANIZATIONS HELPING THE HOMELESS

**Common Cents New York, Inc.**, 500 Eighth Avenue, Room 910, New York, NY 10018. Telephone: (212) 736-6437. Raises money for the homeless through the collection of pennies.

**Habitat for Humanity**, 419 West Church Street, Americus, GA 31709-3498. Telephone: (912) 924-6935. Volunteers build houses for the homeless and poor in America and other countries.

**National Alliance to End Homelessness, Inc.**, 1518 K Street, NW, Washington, D.C. 20005. Telephone: (202) 638-1526. Finds ways to end homelessness and provides assistance to organizations serving the homeless.

**National Coalition for the Homeless, Inc.**, 1621 Connecticut Avenue, NW, Washington, D.C. 20009. Telephone: (202) 265-2371. Works for and assists the homeless.

**Reading is Fundamental** (see page 120).

**The Salvation Army National Headquarters**, P.O. Box 269, Alexandria, VA 22313. Telephone: (703) 684-5500. An international organization that provides shelter for the homeless and feeds the hungry.

**Second Harvest** (see page 116).

## SOME ORGANIZATIONS HELPING THE HUNGRY

**American Jewish World Service, Inc.**, 15 West 26th Street, 9th floor, New York, NY 10010. Telephone: (212) 683-1161. Dedicated to helping the hungry and needy in poor countries.

**Bread for the World, Inc.**, and Bread for the World Institute on Hunger and Development, 802 Rhode Island Avenue, NE, Washington, D.C. 20018. Telephone: (202) 269-0200. Dedicated to easing world hunger.

**Care USA** (see page 116).

**Catholic Relief Services**, 209 West Fayette Street, Baltimore, MD 21202. Telephone: (301) 625-2220. Assists the poor in countries other than the United States and provides disaster relief.

**Food for the Hungry**, 7729 East Greenway Road, Scottsdale, AZ 85260. Telephone: (609) 998-3100 or (800)2-HUNGER. Provides disaster relief and self-help support to the hungry.

**Food Works**, 64 Main Street, Montpelier, VT 05602. Telephone: (802) 223-1515. Feeds the hungry through community and school gardens.

**The Freedom From Hunger Foundation, Inc.**, 1644 Da Vinci Court, Davis, CA 95617. Telephone: (916) 758-6200. Develops solutions to world hunger problem.

**Ox Fam America**, 115 Broadway, Boston, MA 02116. Telephone: (617) 482-1211. Provides famine relief and teaches people in poor countries how to grow their own food.

**The Salvation Army**, (see above).

**Second Harvest, the National Food Bank Network**, 116 Michigan Avenue, Suite 4, Chicago, IL 60603. Telephone: (312) 263-2303. A network of food banks, distributing food to homeless shelters, day-care and senior citizen centers, soup kitchens, and others.

**World Mercy Fund**, 121 South Saint Asaph Street, Alexandria, VA 22314. Telephone: (703) 548-4646. Works to help the hungry and poor throughout the world, especially Africa.

## SOME ORGANIZATIONS PROVIDING DISASTER RELIEF

**American National Red Cross**, 18th and D Streets, Washington, D.C. 20006. Telephone: (202) 737-8300. Provides food, shelter, and other help for people in countries hit by disasters. Helps avoid, prepare, and cope with health emergencies.

**American Friends Service Committee**, 1501 Cherry Street, Philadelphia, PA 19102. Telephone: (215) 241-7000. Provides disaster relief around the world, promotes non-violence and world peace.

**AmeriCares Foundation, Inc.**, 161 Cherry Street, New Canaan, CT 06840. Telephone: (203) 966-5195 or (800) 486-HELP. An international organization providing long-term medical and emergency disaster relief around the world.

**Care USA**, 660 First Avenue, New York, NY 10016. Telephone: (212) 686-3110. Provides international emergency and disaster relief. Also dedicated to helping the world's poor people support themselves.

**Catholic Relief Services** (see page 115).

**Direct Relief International**, 27 South La Patera Lane, Santa Barbara, CA 93117. Telephone: (805) 964-4767. Provides medical assistance to people in disaster areas throughout the world.

**Food for the Hungry** (see page 115).

# SOME ORGANIZATIONS HELPING THE SICK AND DISABLED

**Alexander Graham Bell Association for the Deaf, Inc.**, 3417 Volta Place, NW, Washington, D.C. 20007. Telephone: (202) 337-5220 or (800) 255-4817. Promotes the teaching of language, speech, and lipreading to the deaf. Also works for better educational facilities for deaf children.

**American Foundation for the Blind, Inc.**, 15 West 16th Street, New York, NY 10011. Telephone: (212) 620-2000 or (212) 620-2158. Creates and runs programs that help blind and visually impaired people lead independent lives.

**American National Red Cross** (See page 116)

**Association for Retarded Citizens of the United States**, 500 East Border Street, Suite 300, Arlington, TX 76010. Telephone: (817) 261-6003. Works to promote the well-being of all persons who are retarded, to prevent retardation, and to search for cures.

**Braille Institute of America, Inc.**, 741 North Vermont Avenue, Los Angeles, CA 90029. Telephone: (213) 663-1111. Provides free education and training to blind and visually impaired people.

**Canine Companions for Independence**, P.O. Box 446, Santa Rosa, CA 95402. Telephone: (707) 528-0830. Trains and gives dogs to be helpmates to the disabled.

**Children's Quilt Project**, 1478 University Avenue, Suite 186, Berkeley, CA 94702. Telephone: (510) 548-3843. Makes quilts to give to children with AIDS.

**Disability Rights Education and Defense Fund Inc.**, 2212 Sixth Street, Berkeley, CA 94710. Telephone: (510) 644-2555 or (510) 644-2629. Helps people with physical handicaps live independently.

**Goodwill Industries of America Inc.**, 9200 Wisconsin Avenue, Bethesda, MD 20814-3896. Telephone: (301) 530-6500. Provides leadership and education to help the disabled.

**Guide Dog Foundation for the Blind, Inc.**, 371 East Jericho Turnpike, Smithtown, NY 11787. Telephone: (800) 548-4337. Trains and gives blind people seeing eye dogs.

**Guiding Eyes for the Blind, Inc.**, 611 Granite Springs Road, Yorktown Heights, NY 10598. Telephone: (914) 245-4024. Trains and gives blind people seeing eye dogs.

**Helen Keller International, Inc.**, 15 West 16th Street, New York, NY 10011. Telephone: (212) 807-5800. Works to prevent blindness and to help blind people in poor countries.

**The Hole-in-the-Wall Gang Camp Fund**, 555 Long Wharf Drive, New Haven, CT 06511. Telephone: (203) 772-0522. A special camp for kids with serious health problems.

**Make-a-Wish Foundation**, 2600 North Central Avenue, Suite 936, Phoenix, AZ 85016. Telephone: (800) 722-9474. Fulfills the wishes of very ill kids.

**National Information Center for Children and Youth with Disabilities**, P.O. Box 1492, Washington, D.C. 20013. Telephone: (800) 999-5599. Answers questions regarding children with disabilities.

**Project Concern International**, 3550 Afton Road, San Diego, CA 92123. Telephone: (619) 279-9690. Provides free medical care for kids all over the world.

**Recording for the Blind**, 20 Roszel Road, Princeton, NJ 08540. Telephone: (800) 221-4792. Records and provides free textbooks and educational material to the blind.

**Shriners Hospital for Crippled Children**, P.O. Box 31356, Tampa, FL 33631-3356. Telephone: (800) 237-5055; in Florida: (800) 282-9161. A network of hospitals offering free special medical care to kids.

**Special Olympics International**, 1350 New York Avenue, Suite 500, NW, Washington, D.C. 20005. Telephone: (202) 628-3630. Organizes regional and national athletic competitions for the disabled and retarded.

**Starlight Foundation**, 12233 West Olympic Boulevard, Los Angeles, CA 90064. Telephone: (310) 207-5558. Fulfills the wishes of very ill kids.

*Keep in mind:* Maybe you're interested in helping fight a specific disease. Cancer, diabetes, muscular dystrophy, etc... There are a number of organizations dedicated to fighting diseases like this. Too many to list here. Look for them in your telephone book or ask your doctor, parent, or teacher.

## SOME ORGANIZATIONS HELPING THE ELDERLY

**Catholic Charities USA** (see page 114).

**Four-One-One**, (see page 114).

**Jewish Association for the Services for the Aged**, 40 West 68th Street, New York, NY 10023. Telephone: (212) 724-3200. Amongst its activities, it runs and oversees nursing homes and senior citizens centers.

**National Council on Aging**, 400 Third Street, SW, Suite 200, Washington, D.C. 20024. Telephone: (202) 479-1200. Works to improve the lives of older people.

**Salvation Army** (see page 115).

**United Way** (see page 114).

**Volunteers of America** (see page 114).

# SOME ORGANIZATIONS HELPING KIDS

**American National Red Cross** (See page 116).

**CARE USA** (See page 116).

**Child Find of America**, P.O. Box 277, New Paltz, NY 12561-9277. Telephone: (914) 255-1848. Helps find missing or kidnapped children.

**Child Welfare League of America**, 440 First Street, NW, Suite 310, Washington, D.C. 20001. Telephone: (202) 638-2952. Works to improve the lives of abused, troubled, and neglected children.

**Children's Aid International**, 1420 Third Avenue, Suite 224, San Diego, CA 90048. Telephone: (800) 842-2810. Works to relieve the suffering of poor kids throughout the world.

**Children's Quilt Project** (See page 117).

**Christian Children's Fund**, 2821 Emery Wood Parkway, P.O. Box 26511, Richmond, VA 23261-6511. Telephone: (800) 776-6767. Has an adoption program and offers help to poor kids throughout the world.

**Fresh Air Fund**, 1040 Avenue of the Americas, New York, NY 10018. Telephone: (212) 221-0900 or (800) 367-0003. Sends city kids to "camp" at other people's homes or to one of their special summer camps.

**Kids Against Crime**. (see page 113).

**National Association for the Prevention of Child Abuse**, 332 S. Michigan Avenue, Suite 1600, Chicago, IL 60604. Telephone: (312) 663-3520. Works to prevent all forms of child abuse.

**National Center for Missing and Exploited Children**, 2101 Wilson Boulevard, Suite 550, Arlington, VA 22201. Telephone: (703) 235-3900. Operates a toll free hotline (800) 843-5678 for reporting information on missing kids. Also provides help in finding missing or kidnapped kids.

**National Information Center for Children and Youth with Disabilities**, (see page 118).

**Pearl S. Buck Foundation**, Box 181, Perkasie, PA 18944. Telephone: (800) 220-2825. Has an adoption program, helps kids throughout the world with an emphasis on Asia.

**Plan International, USA**, 155 Plan Way, Warwick, RI 02866. Telephone: (800) 556-7918. Has an adoption program and offers help to poor kids throughout the world.

**Project Concern International** (see page 118).

**Reading is Fundamental**, 600 Maryland Avenue, SW, Washington, D.C. 20560. Telephone: (202) 287-3220. Promotes literacy; it's Open Book program provides homeless children with books and reading centers. Among its other activities, it brings the gift of books and literacy to at-risk children in needy communities.

**Save The Children**, 54 Wilton Road, P.O. Box 940, Westport, CT 06881. Telephone: (800) 243-5075. In addition to its adoption program, it has a variety of programs to help poor kids throughout the world.

**Shriners Hospital for Crippled Children** (See page 118).

**Special Olympics**, (see page 118).

**U.S. Committee for Unicef**, 333 East 38th Street, New York, NY 10016. Telephone: (212) 686-5522. A United Nations organization dedicated to serving poor kids throughout the world. The U.S. committee raises money to support its efforts.

## SOME ORGANIZATIONS HELPING THE PLANET AND ANIMALS

**Adopt-a-Stream Foundation**, P.O. Box 5558, Everett, WA 98206. Telephone: (206) 388-3487. Provides guidelines to the public for "adopting" a stream or wetland.

**American Oceans Campaign**, 725 Arizona Avenue, Suite 102, Santa Monica, CA 90401. Telephone: (310) 576-6162.

**American Society for the Prevention of Cruelty to Animals (ASPCA)**, 424 East 92nd Street, New York, NY 10128. Telephone: (212) 876-7700 or (212) 876-7711. Works to prevent cruelty to animals; maintains shelters for homeless animals.

**Animal Welfare Institute**, P.O. Box 3650, Washington, D.C. 20007. Telephone: (202) 337-2332. Works for the humane treatment of laboratory animals and the development of non-animal testing, the preservation of threatened species, and stopping cruel trapping methods.

**Center for Environmental Information**, 46 Prince Street, Rochester, NY 14607. Telephone: (716) 271-3550. Provides information to the public; specialists in acid rain.

**Center for Marine Conservation**, Suite 500, 1725 De Sales Street, NW, Washington, D.C. 20036. Telephone: (202) 429-5609. Protects marine mammals and fisheries against pollution; helps legislators write laws that affect marine life, and helps citizens voice their concerns to legislators.

**Citizens' Clearing House for Hazardous Waste**, P.O. Box 6806, Falls Church, VA 22040. Telephone: (703) 276-7070. Answers questions regarding hazardous waste; provides handbooks and how-to information to the public.

**The Costeau Society**, 870 Greenbrier Circle, Suite 402, Chesapeake, VA 23320-2641. Telephone: (804) 523-9335. Conducts research and programs on conservation and protection of the environment.

**Defenders of Wildlife, Inc.**, 1244 19th Street, NW, Washington, D.C. 20036. Telephone: (202) 659-9510. Works to prevent the extinction of animals and plants throughout the world.

**Ducks Unlimited**, One Waterfowl Way, Long Grove, IL 60047-9153. Telephone: (708) 438-4300. Works to protect waterfowl (ducks and other birds) and the wetlands, the places where they live and nest. "Greenwing" is the name of their kids group.

**Earth Island Institute**, 300 Broadway, Suite #28, San Francisco, CA 94133-3312. Telephone: (415) 788-3666. Educates the public and develops materials for schools on environmental issues. Sponsors activists projects such as "The Dolphin Project," "The Sea Turtle Restoration Project."

**Environmental Action, Inc.**, 6930 Carroll Avenue, Suite 600, Takoma Park, MD 20912. Telephone: (301) 891-1100. Founded by the organizers of the first Earth Day, works to eliminate environmental toxins and global warming, reduce solid wastes, promote recycling, and improve air quality.

**Environmental Defense Fund, Inc.**, 257 Park Avenue South, 16th Floor, New York, NY 10010. Telephone: (212) 505-2100. Protects the environment through scientific research, lobbying, and public education.

**The Fund for Animals, Inc.**, 200 West 57th Street, Suite 508, New York, NY 10019. Telephone: (212) 246-2096. Works to protect wildlife and fight cruelty to animals through education and legal action. Runs animal shelters.

**Global Releaf Program**, American Forest, P.O. Box 2000, Washington, D.C. 20013. Telephone: (800) 368-5748. Provides information on trees and how to grow them.

**Greenpeace USA, Inc.**, 1436 U Street, NW, Washington, D.C. 20009. Telephone: (202) 462-1177. Works for ocean conservation and wildlife ecology and against nuclear proliferation and toxins. The Humane Society of the United States, 2100 L Street, NW, Washington, D.C. 20037. Telephone: (202) 452-1100. Promotes the humane treatment of animals, with an emphasis on spaying programs.

**Keep America Beautiful**, Mill River Plaza, 9 West Broad Street, Stamford, CT 06902. Telephone: (203) 323-8987. Educates the public about litter and pollution. Helps organizations and individuals clean up their community.

**Kids Against Pollution (KAP)**, (see page 113).

**Kids For Saving Earth**, (see page 113).

**National Arbor Day Foundation**,100 Arbor Avenue, Nebraska City, NE 68410. Telephone: (402) 474-5655. Provides tree seedlings and information on how to grow them.

**National Audubon Society, Inc.**, 950 Third Avenue, New York, NY 10012. Telephone: (212) 832-3200. Its interests include ecology, energy conservation, restoration of natural resources, with a particular emphasis on wildlife, wildlife habitats, soil, water, and forests.

**National Humane Education Society, Inc.**, 15-B Catoctin Circle, SE, Room 207, Leesburg, VA 22075. Telephone: (703) 777-8319. Engages in animal rescue efforts and education programs throughout the country.

**National Recycling Coalition**, 1101 30th Street, NW, Suite 305, Washington, D.C. 20007. Telephone: (202) 625-6406. Provides information on recycling.

**National Wildlife Federation**, 1400 16th Street, NW, Washington, D.C. 20036. Telephone: (202) 797-6800. Works to educate the public about conservation and the symptoms of and solutions to environmental abuse. Runs the Backyard Wildlife Program.

**The Nature Conservancy**, 1815 North Lynn Street, Arlington, VA 22209. Telephone (703) 841-5300. Works to prevent the destruction of endangered animals by preserving protected habitats where they can survive.

**New York Zoological Society**, Bronx, NY 10460-1099. Telephone: (212) 220-5100. Its Sponsor-A-Species program works to save endangered animals.

**Rainforest Action Network**, 450 Sansome Street, Suite 700, San Francisco, CA 94111. Telephone: (415) 398-4404.

**Save-the-Redwoods League**, 114 Sansome Street, Room 605, San Francisco, CA 94104. Telephone: (415) 362-2352. Buys private redwood and sequoia forest to add to the park system so it will be preserved forever.

**Sierra Club**, 730 Polk Street, San Francisco, CA 94109. Telephone: (415) 776-2211. Works to protect the environment with an emphasis on global warming.

**TreePeople**, 12601 Mulholland Drive, Beverly Hills, CA 90210. Telephone: (818) 769-2663. Plants smog- and disease-resistant trees.

**Trees for Life**, 1103 Jefferson Street, Wichita, KS 67203. Telephone: (316) 263-7294. Provides information and advice on planting and growing trees.

**The Wilderness Society**, 900 17th Street, NW, Washington, D.C. 20006. Telephone: (202) 833-2300. Devoted to issues relating to the preservation and proper management of America's wilderness and public lands.

**World Wildlife Fund**, 1250 24th Street, Suite 500, NW, Washington, D.C. 20037. Telephone: (202) 293-4800. Works to protect endangered wildlife and tropical forests mainly in Latin America, Africa, and Asia.

## ABOUT THE AUTHOR

Suzanne Logan is a freelance writer who lives in New York City. She has worked with a variety of volunteer groups and is the mother of two daughters.